Committing to
Lonely

Lori,
You are awesome!
Keep up the counselling ☺

-Pamela

Committing to Lonely

After *'I Do'*

BY

Pamela Grace

Bookstand Publishing
www.BookstandPublishing.com

Published by
Bookstand Publishing
Morgan Hill, CA 95037
3716_2

ISBN 978-1-61863-349-1

Printed in the United States of America

Acknowledgements

To my son and family for their patience and support; their love when I most needed it and their faith in me.

I dedicate this book to the many people who find themselves in a similar lifestyle. May they find ears willing to listen and hearts willing to care.

Table of Contents

Prologue

Where was I? My thoughts were falling as fast and hard as the rain on the dirty window I was looking through. The flashes of lightning emanated the streaming water trails rushing down the glass. It looked as if the rain was unsuccessfully trying to wash the years of built up dirt off the once clear window panes. Darkness and silence filled the gaps between crashes of thunder. My eyes never left the view of an empty blackness out the window. Staring out into nothingness, I allowed my unmoving body to absorb the feeling of anguish the storm was giving me.

Cry, I silently told the night. Cry for me, I have no tears left. Please, I begged the storm; feel for me.... Feel what I no longer am able to feel. Mourn and shed millions of tears. Try if you will to wash away the sorrow and emptiness that has consumed me. Pour out all the emotions that have drowned my laughter and murdered my sense of who I was. Unleash on this earth your contempt for things that are unfair and hurtful. Give misery to those who have made me miserable.

Dear God, is that you hurting for me? Have you seen what I am living in and with? You said when I cry you would cry with me. Is this your way of crying with me....crying for me?

The storm responded in anger as it brought strong winds out of nowhere. The thunder crashed and the house moved with its vibrations. The wind increased its volume outside, pushing against the house. In some way even the night storm was rejecting my plea for oneness with something. I heard the wind screaming at me, angry that I would dare try to assume it was here as an ally of mine. "YOU ARE ALONE.... NO ONE WANTS TO BE WITH YOU.....YOU DON'T DESERVE LOVE!"

Words …..they never stop!

"You stupid bitch….you SLUT…..go shit yourself!"

Somehow the rain was not washing away 'the words' that swirled around in my head. The thunder was not loud enough to make me not hear 'the words'. The lightning was not bright enough to blind me of the mental images that would not stop playing over and over again in front of my mind's eye.

"The storm was not enough God," I whimpered to Him.

Only when the lightning flashed could I see that the trees were waving their branches madly about. What did they want? Did they think if they moved enough they could pick themselves up from where they were and run from this storm?

Every time the lightning flashed I could see them still rooted to their spots, unmoved; their desire alone to run away was not enough. My stone heart felt a slight twinge of remorse for the trees. "You can't go anywhere;" I whispered sadly at the black window in between lit moments. "If you move….you will die. Is this what you are waiting for? Do you think that death is better than standing through this storm? Don't break! Stand and take this storm, it is going to pass and there will be a better day."

Why was I giving hope to something that knew nothing? I sucked in a little breath and held it for a moment. Did that mean there was still hope for me? That there was still hope *in* me? I held that thought for a moment longer and with amazement, let it slowly emerge clearly out of the anger and resentment surrounding my soul. It was like looking at a small lit candle through the heavy bars of a dank and stinking black, cold prison cell. Yet, it was hope and it ever so slightly warmed my soul with a small shimmer of light.

FLASH! The lightning showed me evidence that the trees had not won their struggle to get free of the storm. CRASH! The thunder shook the foundation of the house. HOOOWWWWWWWWLLL! The wind wailed it's furry around the creaking structure that tried to shelter me.

How did I get to be here? What happened? Why could I sit and not move for hours and just stare at nothing? When did I change into a piece of useless flesh, with no purpose to exist other than to satiate one other human being? A human being that needed someone to wipe his feet on and then demand his slippers be fetched at the end of his "hard" day. A person that told me when I could speak, for how long I was allowed to and when I had to shut my mouth and not mutter a single word? Someone that told me what conversations he would accept from me, and in what direction my thoughts could go. I was manipulated and controlled by his selfish temper tantrums. I was in need of "SEVERE" reprimand that could take hours if in any way shape or form I did not think his way, or read his mind fast enough.

Yes, I had never been good at reading someone's mind. Was there a course I could have taken growing up, that I missed?

I was under an allusion that people had generally gotten along with me. I loved people, and enjoyed taking care of others. Listening to them tell me of their hurts and frustrations, as many had come to a point in their life where they had been stripped of their independence and lived with pain. I have worked in the health care field in the community and hospitals for many years. I enjoyed showing others that a gentle and caring person was taking care of them. I wanted ...no, needed to care for people. There was no other job that would give me satisfaction in life. It was not about the money. I was not a nurse and did not make a very big wage. Yet, I took care of and loved people with special needs and the elderly as if my own heart needed to love them in order to keep beating. I fell in love with many "grandma's and grandpa's" that came and went in my working hours. I regret nothing. I felt them and their families loved me back, what more could you want in life?

I turned my head in the darkened house and assessed the table I was sitting at. The lights in the house were not on for the power had gone out some time ago. I stared at the dark shape of my husband's lap top computer, his calculator and some papers. Do I dare move anything on the table? I could, but if I moved it to a spot that my husband had to look for it...then I would get into trouble. If I left his things were they sat on the table but should have put them away....then I would get into trouble. If he forgot (which he does quite often), that "he" had left them on the table, therefore force him to look for them; then he would give me trouble anyway demanding where his things are assuming that I had moved them.

So what should I do? Another flash of light lit up the house for a second, as I turned back to stare out the window in time to see nothing but black again.

In my mind, I walked over to the closet in our bedroom and picked up my little back pack, threw some things into it and phoned for a ride to the woman's shelter that I was told to go to. In my mind I struggled with the "what should I take" scenario, I have gone through a million times. I have no money anymore. I don't know anything about my finances and have never seen "the bank account". We have a joint account that he will put enough money into for any given small task that I might be sent on. Such as picking some groceries up at the store or ..... well, there really is no "or". The amount put in the account will be calculated by how much groceries will cost and that is what will be transferred from "his" account to our "joint" account. He knew how to calculate the amount needed because his mom worked in a grocery store for years while he was growing up. He had a fixation on prices. He was the only man I knew that absolutely had to know a price for something or read flyers like they were a newspaper. If it wasn't in a flyer, then he would search the internet. He has to know prices and I learned when shopping with him, I had to ask…..'is this a good price?'

He does all the paying of bills and other errands a household would do to keep functioning. You know I am not able to do these things. He told me that if he didn't do them they would not be done or worse would not be done right!

Everything is in his name. He bought a small hobby farm and made sure that my name was not on the papers anywhere. He has told me with violent words over and over again that "THIS HOUSE IS HIS!!!" The animals are his, the camper trailer is his and so is the quad and car. I do have a truck though. It is an old, white Chevy that is sitting with no plates in the yard, needing a transmission amongst probably other things, collecting rust and spider webs. Yes, the truck is mine. I could not see it now for the storms dark rage hid it from me. Yet, I know it is still out there somewhere sitting alone just like its owner inside the house.

I could leave. Then what? I can't stop asking myself this question. I don't have the answer and I fear it may be too late anyway. I could take my small back pack, walk out the door and never look back. Walk away from everything. My son (thank you Jesus), is 21 and on his own so that is not stopping me. So, what is?

….I said 'for better or worse'…..

Maybe the fairy tale dream I had of a marriage to a man that I loved and had thought that he loved me back. Someone that would stand by my side in those times of life that it felt the world was against me. Someone, who would not allow another person to swear at or hurt me physically. A man, who wanted to walk out his dreams with me, plan goals, and pursue small pleasures you may find along life's path. I never thought that I would have a marriage that did not have disagreements in it. I knew enough that every couple I have seen or knew of would not agree on everything. Yet, I imagined that my husband and I would always be able to "agree to disagree" without violence. I thought that I could make my husband happy and he could make me happy in return, for the better part of our union. Not with material things but by being each other's best friend.

I sucked in a deep breath of regret and instantly felt a quick sharp pain in my front tooth. My front tooth always reminded me it was not real when something cool, sweet or too hot would touch it.

I will never forget the look in his eyes when he broke it. Or the words he said to me. I will never forget that he seemed to be pleased when he seen that I was bleeding, almost like he had achieved a win. He has never said "sorry for hurting you" to me. Instead, when that night or the others are brought up, he screams at me in complete rage and disgust that he was arrested because of me. Everything was and still is my fault. He is the victim in our marriage. It is his rite to personally correct my stupidity and let me know the facts of who I am. I am the stupidest person on this earth that he has ever met. I am the worst slut in the world. (Well, according to him ALL women are sluts with the only exception being his mommy. She is perfect.) I am the worst bitch and meanest person he has ever known of and I deserve not only when he yells at me or hurts me but I deserve it if and when others do the same. His mom screamed and yelled at me too that night. She was allowed. I deserved it. I "need" to be spoken to in a manner to which you would an absolute idiot. I wouldn't understand anything else you see. I am a useless waist of ignorant, lazy mass. I don't have needs, just make him happy; don't 'piss' him off…. and I will survive.

The wind started to silence its aggressive movements outside. The intensity and frequency of the lightning and thunder abated. Now the rain could be heard again but not seen as it continued trying to wash the dirty windows. The electricity came back on and I could now only see the reflection of me sitting alone at the kitchen table in the black window.

"How did you handle the storm trees?" Tears welled up in my eyes, letting me know that I did have some left in me to shed. "Did you gain your freedom from the storm?" I waited for another now infrequent flash of light to see how they did. The wait seemed forever as the storm quieted. I now could hear the ticking clock on the kitchen wall in the next room, which made time passing almost painful.

The flash happened and for a brief moment I could see trees standing where they were supposed to be. Their branches hanging tired all around them, some broken. But….the trees were still there.

"The storm wanted to destroy you trees. Yet you are still there. A little bruised and broken, but not fallen. I told you there was still hope after a storm. This has made you stronger; it has gotten rid of your week members and strengthened your roots. You survived this night. Breath and rest trees, until the next storm hits …breath and rest. I too will survive this and I will use the stone that was meant to break me as a stepping stone, it will make me stronger too."

I mentally walked into the bedroom and once again packed my back pack. Without moving I stared blankly at the phone to make that call. Nothing happened, I did not move. The only sounds were the ticking of the kitchen clock, now far away thunder and soft rain that had lightened its attack on the window pain.

How long had the storm lasted? How long did I sit staring out a black window? How long will this last?

Head lights came and illuminated the gravel driveway outside showing me the trees, barn and fenced area surrounding it. Letting me know that he had finally arrived home from who knows where and who knows who with. Like a faithful doggy I prepared myself to greet the master of the house. Will he talk to me or will he slam things around and dare me to piss him off? I don't have to guess if he is going to share any small talk with me.

I exhaled, rubbed the back of my neck and stretched my shoulders back then pushed myself away from the table by the window. I glanced down at the phone that was still in the same spot and looked back towards the bedroom where I knew my back pack was still in the closet empty. "Next time for real", I promised myself. I won't sit through another storm in this house. My heart knew exactly what my brain just said. It could happen soon, maybe not soon enough or too soon….I won't know until the moment that I walk out the door and close it firmly behind me. I won't know until then.

The door opened bringing my husband into view. He looked at me with disgust as if to let me know that he was in no way pleased at looking at me or being in the same room with me.

When will this end? When will the 'worse' part of the marriage end? It began right after we both said…………."for better or worse"…………"in sickness and health"…….. it began four years ago………..

"How was your day?" I said without emotion. Maybe…..for the last time.

1

Before 'I do'

Tears were welling up in my eyes and my cheeks had already been hurting for the past 20 minutes from laughing at my son's stories. He had just come back from babysitting a long time friend's two young boys. My son Jason was 17, in grade 12 and held a maturity that soared above his peers.

The two boys he had been babysitting for the past several months just loved him and he, in return, loved being with them. The antics that took place in the hours of them being together were worth several extremely funny stories once he returned home.

We were sitting at the dinner table in my Kelowna condo on a warm fall evening, enjoying an animated conversation. Laughing constantly at the silly manner in which we could both recount something that had transpired in our day apart from each other. Neither of us had too much to complain about. Life was good and living in our home town close to all our family and friends was worth feeling satisfied with life.

We finished our stories and I got up to start the clean up after supper. Moving to the kitchen sink with the two plates empty now of food, I smiled again still thinking of the "knitting needle" story he had just told me when he came back out of his room.

"Mom, dad just sent me an email". He told me with hesitation in his voice watching my response.

"Great," I thought what a way to ruin my night. I didn't share this thought with him but I was fully aware that no matter what I said or didn't say my son knew how I felt.

Mack was a dad that had never been there for his son. I became pregnant after I had gotten really sick and had to go on amoxicillin that "may or may not counteract the birth control pill". Well, it counteracted with me. I was blessed beyond words because God had allowed me to mother this wonderful person who was my son. How unfortunate that his dad in his selfishness was unable to have enjoyed any of our son's life so far.

I had broken up with him because I knew that being faithful was not a part of his makeup. We met in Banff in the summer when I was 17 and had a summer romance that we (or I) thought was going to last forever. I had gotten fired for having him in the staff house with me, so I left Banff and moved back to BC. He stayed in Banff to finish his summer off working there. The fact that I was fired because of him didn't seem to affect him. What did I want him to do? Maybe stand up for me or tell me he loved me so much that he wanted to quit his summer job to spend the last couple weeks of his vacation with me? Ah, the dreams of a young girl in love hm? I know now they were just that....dreams. After the summer was over he moved back to Quebec. He stopped in to see me for a quick two day camping trip before continuing his journey home.

He had gone to Banff with his girlfriend (that I did not know he had when we started dating), to learn to speak better English. He was my prince charming, sort of. I never really believed in fairy tales but he was tall, dark and handsome with what seemed to be a gentle manner and an eagerness to be with me and experience life with me. We promised to stay together even though we lived so far apart. We said we would visit each other until our schooling was finished then I would move to Quebec to be with him. This was the plan. After two months of being apart I had saved up what money I could from working part time and went to visit him via greyhound. For two weeks I stayed with his family and visited many different parts of Montréal and surrounding areas. I met with several of his family members and loved them all. I could not speak French and they could barely speak English yet we seemed to get along fine in our broken conversations. But......there were a couple instances that shattered the imagined perfect relationship I had with Mack that would haunt me many years later in life.

One night he decided to take me to an old English pub in downtown Montreal. So, together with one of his school friends we sat down at a table, ordered a drink and they talked. I sat there like a lump but was ok with this because I was sitting next to him. My left leg was resting over his right one and his arm was around me. Then, out of the crowded pub came two women our age. They came up to where Mack was sitting, speaking French and one of them looked at me, grabbed my leg and shoved it off of Mack's so she could sit down in his lap. He immediately removed his arm from around me and placed it around her. They were laughing and talking in a flirting manner as I sat there stunned.

He was enjoying this attention and did nothing about what she had just done to me. When I realized this was not going to end soon, I pushed my way out from the table and went to the girl's washroom. Once there I screamed and yelled what an idiot I was for being with someone that would allow that. I thought he loved me? Who was this other girl, and why was she so intimately affectionate with him? The realization that Mack was not lacking affection while we were apart, hit me as I knew that the girl on his lap was more than just an acquaintance. He slept with other girls when he wanted to and did not let being "in a relationship" stop him. Just like he had done with me in Banff. When I found out he had a girlfriend after a month of dating him in Banff, he; with no real emotion told me that he loved her and liked me. Simple as that, no remorse at cheating on her or hurting me. That's how he felt so "suck it up and accept it".

After I found out about the 'girlfriend' he had in Banff, I ended the relationship with him. Yet within a few days he was back in my life letting me know he loved me and that the "girlfriend" had gone back to Quebec. He wanted me, and I believed him. I even believed she left. Sigh....young love hm?

Well, this girl in the English pub was definitely someone that knew his bed. I went back to the table demanding in clear strong English that I was leaving with or without him. He laughed at me and said, as if to a small child that was having a temper tantrum, "We can leave Tammy". He said something to his friend in french and while both of them were laughing, we all left the pub and drove back to his parents' house.

I was hurt. He laughed like he did when once we were passing by an English prostitute and she started calling to him and telling me to "go home little girl, it was past my bedtime". He thought something that puffed his ego up and hurt mine was amusing. He never pulled me closer to him or showed that he was more interested in me than anyone else as I thought a man should. He never made me feel like anything other than an amusing girl from the west that he can "play" with but not be serious about. He never made me feel important to him. He made me feel like I should be thanking God that HE would put such a good looking and wanted by many women 'man' in my life. He considered himself a 'trophy' for any woman. He never showed me that he was happy that 'I' was brought into his life. No, there were many more and better looking women out there wanting him......I was just one......and not one that was really even that interesting or important to him at that.

When I left Montreal on the greyhound to make the four and a half day ride home; I cried. This was the first time I would cry for something I thought I had with him, yet little did I even imagine that this was nothing compared to how much grief and tears I would shed later on in my life because of him.

We kept in touch and he continued to tell me in letters how much he loved me and how much he missed me and that I was the only girl he loved. He was going to show me how much he meant this by coming to BC to visit me over the Christmas season.

Well, he came for the visit all packed and ready for a fun filled ski vacation in Lake Louise......without me. I was getting over a very bad cold and miserable that all those letters about him missing me seemed to have been written by someone else. He came for a vacation, not to see me. A vacation I let him go and have without me. Why did he have to lie to me and let me believe he loved me? Let me wait for him and our / my dream of being together sharing that love?

I held him for the last time as we lay together in my little apartment. I held my dream of a first love for just a few more moments until it was almost time for him to catch his flight to go. Go, to his party and ski vacation. I held him after waiting for what seemed like forever to see him....be with him ......plan for a whole week to be with the man I loved and missed. Only to find out that his plan was to be without me. His plan was to "have fun". His plan was to go ski in the mountains, not come visit me after being apart for several months. I held him for a moment and then, when he got up to put his things together after only spending two days with me, before his "real" vacation; I said goodbye. I knew he did not stop loving other girls just because we were supposed to have been faithful to each other. I knew he did not need my "permission" to have sex with anyone else. Yet, I had to say goodbye to him aloud, I had to say it ….for me. I had to let him continue his life seeking only what gave him pleasure and not thinking about anyone else. He didn't need to be set free, but I did. Of waiting for someone that said one thing and lived another way.

I may have been young, just 18, yet I had lived enough life I felt, to understand what commitment and responsibility meant. He had neither, nor cared to find those qualities at this point in his life. He was all about image and vanity…..and loved it too much to want morals to interfere with his life. So, I watched him get into the taxi with all his ski bags after ending a "true love" relationship, with an eagerness on his face to continue his vacation. A vacation with no girlfriend, filled with parties, skiing and sex with new girls. I was devastated. The first man I loved was walking away…….showing me he really didn't have feelings for me, if he ever had to begin with.

That would have been the last of him except I found out I was pregnant with his child. When I phoned him a couple months later, he was annoyed and told me to have an abortion. Had he told others to do that? Well, this was a life I already loved. I felt no child was a "mistake", and even though I was alone and absolutely terrified of the thought of raising a child on my own…..I was going to do it. I would change my plans of traveling the world and instead learn how to be a mom.

My little boy and I had many adventures. He lived through different babysitters as I struggled to get an education in the health care field. He went without so much because I just did not make enough money to do anything other than pay rent and get just enough groceries, (of which sometimes I needed help from the food bank for)to get through the month with. He was so precious and filled my life with absolute love. He never seemed to complain as the rest of his class mates went on school trips without him because I did not have the money to let him go. He always seemed to place value on spending time with me not what he could get from the store from me. I truly loved the gift God gave me in him. I enjoyed being a mom; it was such an amazing journey to watch this little person experience life at different stages.

As my son looked upon things for the first time, it was like I was also looking at those things new too. A boat ride on the lake, a Jr. hockey game in town, a freshly built snowman, a road trip to Alberta; the west Edmonton mall….the lists were endless and we both soaked life in as much and as often as my budget allowed.

I said yes to getting married to a man when my son was almost 14 months old only to find out that he would do cocaine with his friends once in a while. This was something I did not want to have around my son and who knows if it would get out of hand with this man. I was not willing to go down that road or hurt my son's life by being with someone with an addiction. The second relationship ended by a mother that wanted to send her son back to Germany to find a woman that did not already have a child. At this point, I decided to wait until my son was in grade 12 to look for someone. This would give me time to commit to motherhood and my job without having my son grow up and see different men come and go in his life. I did not want him to get confused with "who was his daddy".

I told Jason about Mack as early as he could understand and showed him pictures so he knew that he had a dad and what he looked like. I would send pictures once in a while to Mack's parents and letters that my son would pretend to write with little scribbles to his dad. I never said anything bad about Mack to Jason. I wanted one day to see that maybe Mack would want to have a relationship with this amazing little boy that just loved so much and smiled so often. After Jason was born, I took him down to Quebec to show Mack and his parents this wonderful little human being, that needed their love. It was not about me. At this point I had lost all respect for such a selfish man and could not believe that I even once loved him. I hated self absorbed people and chose my friends and those that would be part of my life as people that genuinely cared for others. This was not Mack. He only cared if it would benefit him somehow. You could say I had at this point started hating him for not being able to show even a little kindness for such an innocent little person that only wanted to love him in return.

Starting when Jason was about two years old, I would dial the phone, ask for Mack and then hand the phone to Jason so he could wish his dad and grandparents a merry Christmas. By the time Jason was 8, he asked me if we "had to phone" dad at the Christmas season to wish him a merry Christmas because (as Jason put it), "dad doesn't want to talk to me when I phone him". This ended the calls, but I told Jason that it would be nice even once out of every two years to send his grandparents in the east a letter with pictures. You can't blame the grandparents for something the parent was doing, I told him. We made a deal and that is how it was until he turned 15. Up until this point in Jason's life he had never received anything from his grandparents or his dad; not even a dollar store birthday card.

Mack's parents got in touch with us on Jason's 15th year of life to ask to see him. At this point in our lives I was making relatively good money, had purchased a small bungalow, was driving a new car and put every other penny I could save towards a vacation to Disneyland for the two of us every second year. We had also gone to Disneyworld, New Orleans, a cruise on a Disney ship to the Bahamas and several little trips like Drumheller, Jasper and Banff.

If my son wanted to go and meet his grandparents for the first time in his memory, then I would fly him down. Jason wasn't going without me, so tucking my distaste for such selfish people away, I bought two plane tickets and went along with him.

The week went rather well; my son seemed to love the new sites as he did on any one of our vacations. I told Mack's parents that I did not want to "see" Mack at all. We were going down because "they" were the ones showing interest in getting to know their western grandson. Mack showed no interest at all in Jason......after all .....it would interfere with his free little life wouldn't it? Full of no responsibility but to himself and his pleasures. Yet, on one of those evenings before we left, Mack phoned his parents and wanted to take us out for dinner.

US!!! I almost choked on the thought. This trip had not been Mack's idea or wish to see his son and now he wants to take us to dinner? Not me. I asked Jason if he was interested and he was, so I declined and told them that it would be better to just let Jason and his dad have some time alone. So they could get to know each other. I was going to sit downstairs so Mack and I would not have to see each other when he came to pick Jason up for dinner. That was stupid because it turned out to be more like Jason getting to know Mack's girlfriend not his dad.

What a joke that was. Mack's girlfriend was doing all the talking to Jason. Mack didn't say a word! She at one point told Jason that the reason Mack was not talking was because Mack didn't know English that well. When I broke up with Mack over 15 years ago, he knew "a lot" of English! I also knew enough about Mack that the sales job he had now, required a full grasp of the English language!

I was sitting downstairs when I heard that and it took everything in me to stay put and not run up the stairs and tell that woman not to lie to my son. We were not playing any games here so I expected none played in return. I never heard Mack correct her. Why would he? That fell perfectly in line with his character. Don't take responsibility for anything. ALWAYS LET OTHERS FIGHT YOUR BATTLES FOR YOU. ALWAYS HIDE BEHIND SOMEONE ELSE! (I could have vomited with my anger towards such a coward.) Don't show interest in your son or try to find out anything about his life or what he liked or did for interest. 'We came all the way down here at no inconvenience to you out of your pocket or your life; you do not need to lie on top of that!' I let it go and the vacation ended as we flew home two days later with me not having to look at him. Jason finally met his dad and grandparents. That seemed to be good enough for Jason. We could continue our life as usual when we got home.

After my son was almost finished grade eleven, I made a decision. I would go after Mack for child support. Jason was going into grade 12 next year and I wanted Jason to have a wonderful last year in school, being able to go and do anything that came up that I could not be able to pay for. Mack had denied Jason being his son in the courts of Quebec when Jason was an infant and never had to pay for support. I never requested it again. This was different though. I was thinking of Jason. Not of Mack. It was about Jason in his final year of school getting to do what he wanted and not being denied. It was about Jason, getting what he so rightfully deserved.

Remarkably enough, the Family maintenance in BC worked their magic and Mack was sending Jason child support for his final school year. Mack finally admitted a little responsibility for someone other than himself. Not only that but he wanted Jason to come back to Quebec for a visit. This time to do things with him and his girlfriend, not just his parents.

I told Jason that this time would have to be on his dad's dime. I wasn't going to pay again for him to have a relationship with his son. Mack would have to pursue Jason if this is what he wanted. I tried to make a relationship between the two of them for 17 years. It had nothing to do with me. Jason was a young man now and could make his own decisions. Jason could have and build relationships that did not include me. It no longer had to come from or through me. So, just before Jason started grade 12, his dad came to Kelowna to visit his son…..alone.

I was more than shocked at Mack's decision to come alone and spend a whole week with Jason. I made it quite clear that Mack was not going to be staying in my condo; he would definitely have to get his own accommodations. Which he did near the old bridge in downtown Kelowna. He rented a bike and Jason and Mack traveled all over using the bikes. He even went to Jason's sailing lessons with him on the lake.

I did not see Mack for the better part of those days. Still harboring my resentment and guarding my suspicions at why all of a sudden now did he want to acknowledge that he had a son. Trust was not even close to being one of the words I would use in talking to my co-workers about this extreme change of events occurring in my son's life.

Once I learned that Mack had no other children and was just three years away from turning the big 4 0, then this satisfied my curiosity for a time. I told myself that He was having a mid life crisis and knew that Jason was and would ever be his only child.

"So," I told my sister who was just as shocked as I was, "He must want to tell his friends that he too is a dad, just like them."

A couple days left of Mack's visit with Jason was the first time I saw him. I was coming home after work at around eleven p.m. (at which time Jason knew that his dad had to be out of my home), when I saw Mack for the first time face to face.

I parked the car in my stall and slowly turned the engine off. He was walking out of my condo… down the sidewalk…. in front of my car…..in the direction of the road…. our eyes met. There was no reading his expression or mine for that brief moment. 18 years had gone by since we looked into each other's eyes. 18 years. No words, no smiles, no anger……not even a physical twitch of an eyebrow from either of us gave away evidence that we had any emotion what so ever towards one another. He looked like I felt about him. He was way too overly tanned wearing young stylish clothes that screamed "I won't admit to aging". His hair was cut short and full of gel. He held himself with a thick air of vanity wrapped around his "I know you think I am good looking" tilt to his chin. He was the epitome of ego and all about self centeredness wrapped up into a testosterone package. I looked away almost at the same time he did, got out of the car and walked without turning my head in any direction, into the condo.

Once inside, I sat numbly at the table. Hate for such a vain man gave me an instant headache.

"I have to forgive him God", I prayed quietly. "You ask me to forgive others so you can forgive me. Well, I may need your help with this one Father. You know how I feel towards him…..I "need" you to help me. Jesus……help me forgive him".

All of a sudden, a warm sense of peace started at the top of my head and slowly fell through and down my body. It touched my heart and gently started removing the built up anger and resentment against this man from deep within its hiding places.

I never felt anything like it before. I sat unmoving….. waiting…. I didn't know for what but I knew I couldn't move.

My son came back into the house, reached for the phone and said he was going to call the cab company back because it still had not gotten there yet.

"Fine", I said quietly. Then a thought came to me. "God, if this was you helping me to forgive him, then I will drive the man to his hotel and not feel like throwing him into the lake as I pass it".

I felt almost a little smug on that one because I didn't think it was going to happen.

"Oh, ok thank you". My son hung the phone up."The dispatcher with the cab company just told me that the car had already picked a man up on this street. I'll go see if he is gone".

The street was open, it was close to midnight and not too many people were even walking it during that hour. It was a quiet street at its busiest time of day. Mack was the only one out there waiting for a cab. It had to have been him.

"That's too bad," I told Jason as he was opening the door to go out again, "I was just about to offer to drive him to his hotel so he would save a couple dollars". I smiled at his funny expression as he responded to me.

"Yah, sure mom, I'll tell him that if he is still outside".

I stretched at the table enjoying my new freedom from hard feelings, and started thanking God for His awesomeness when Jason came back in even more puzzled than when he left.

"What's wrong", I asked

"Dad is still on the road?" "He never seen any cab come and there has not been anyone else out there this whole time". Jason smiled and said,"…but he accepts your offer of a ride to the hotel".

I looked up toward the ceiling and accepted the fact that God 'did' want me to forgive and I felt like I was going to have to show forgiveness sooner than I ever wanted to. Me and my promise!

I jumped up from the table, grabbed my purse and car keys, looked at my son as we both started for the door and said; "I don't want to talk to him though"! I wanted this over quick.

He was leaning against the passenger side of my nice white Buick. I loved my car. It had plenty of room and was extremely comfortable to ride in. Yet, that evening as I mentally placed a very think, sound proof wall between me and the back seat passenger, it felt somehow smaller than I remembered.

He got out after I parked near the side entrance of the hotel he was staying at and he thanked me for the ride.

"Your welcome", I replied as I would to a complete stranger.

Jason talked outside the car with him for a couple minutes arranging their plans for the next day, said goodbye and got back into the car.

"Can we borrow the car tomorrow?" Jason started telling me about their plans to go biking on an old bike path, but they would need some way of getting there as it was out of town and way too far for them to bike there.

"You are joking right? You want me to lend him my car? You feeling ok?"

"Mom, you're not working tomorrow and it would be nice of you". He gave me his 'cheeky' smile and at that I couldn't resist. 'This is for Jason' I thought.

"OK, you guys can use my car tomorrow". I wanted to spend the day with my sister anyway so we could just go out in her car. I would phone her in the morning and ask her to pick me up. I chuckled to myself imagining what her response to 'why' I needed her to pick me up instead of meet her somewhere, was going to be.

Two days after that, Mack was leaving the hot, sunny Okanogan to go back to Montreal.

He asked Jason if he could spend that day with both of us. Unfortunately I was not working that evening and had no reason other than absolute rudeness to not join them.

It helped to see how happy my son was at finally getting to know his dad. Jason was the most forgiving and loving person I knew. I could do no different than my son. So, I joined them for a go-cart race in Westbank and then later dinner at a restaurant off of Hwy 97.

At this point I really never felt anything for him. No anger, no hate, no joy, no friendliness, no common ground to even talk about other than our son. Jason was taking the transition of having a "dad" in his life smoother than I was at the idea of talking to a person like they somehow 'shared' parental rights.

I felt sorry for his girlfriend back in Quebec when we were standing outside the restaurant that night waiting for a table. Mack was completely smitten by three young ladies also standing outside the restaurant wearing typical summer slim fashions. I almost laughed at him when it looked like he was puffing himself up to get their attention. He could have been shouting at them ….."I really like what I see, how about you girls? Do you like what you see in me?" I shook my head with distaste and again pity for his girlfriend when a wave of memories came over me.

"You have not changed Mack…..your still all about vanity and still think, 'if it's a female….then it must want you'.

We ate dinner and on the drive back to the condo where the two of them were planning to watch a movie, Mack tried telling me a joke about finding a genie and asking the genie for someone that looked like me.

'Yip; poor girlfriend back home.' I don't think Mack knew how to talk to the opposite sex without flirting. It was as much a part of him as his head or feet. I still could not see him ever being faithful to anyone.

He flew back home the next morning and we continued living our lives as before he came down. I continued dating (like I promised myself I would as soon as Jason was in grade 12).

I was happy and so was Jason. He was doing more and more with his friends and I was learning how to enjoy a new life too. A life with my son that no longer needed a mother, as our relationship turned more into friendship.

Jason and his dad were communicating quite a bit via the internet and I found myself sending and receiving emails from Mack also. Mostly, just random forwarded jokes. Or, to share something funny that Jason had done or said. It was strange, yet both Jason and I had completely forgiven Mack and opened our arms…..and our hearts up for him to be welcome in our lives. Of course, Jason never had hated his dad.

One thing that still bothered me though….Mack never talked to Jason about why it took him so long to want to be his dad. Or said "sorry, you know for not being there", or …well, anything. He was acting like he was always there for him and that there was no "great divide".

"Whatever Tammy", I told myself….."Leave it in the past and in the 'forgiven' pile."

I stopped filling the sink with warm soap water to hear what my son wanted to tell me.

"OK," I smiled at my son as he came back into the room after checking his computer for emails. "Your dad sent you an email….what is so news worthy in it that you should let me know about it?" I turned completely away from the dishes in the sink giving my son my full attention, and waited for his response.

2

Rekindled Love

Jason was looking at me with a "what's up" expression.

"He was telling me that he thought you were beautiful and he loved talking to you. He wants to know if you are going to be at your computer tomorrow night when you get off work." He leaned over the kitchen island waiting for a response. A big smile came across his face as he unsuccessfully hid the amusement he somehow found in the news he just presented me.

"I think he still likes you." It was a statement from Jason. He said it as a fact, like he would have just informed me of a grade he got on a test. In a manner of fact style with a 'nothing is going to change it' attitude.

What's wrong with me? I stood like a piece of stone sticking out of the floor. A flood of emotions washed over me swirling around in a confusing furry. Was that excitement I felt? Wait a minute ….no, my stomach was turning like I was going to be sick. Was I going to have a headache? Am I mad? No, were those butterflies jumping around inside of me? Was that joy or anger that just swept past my heart? Was I glad or scared? Why was this news hitting me like this? Why should I care? I may be reading too much into this anyway. It could just mean that he saw me like he would someone he worked with. Yah, that's it. It means that he doesn't hate me….he likes me. No different than someone he works with.

Ok, so that was it. Well what the heck were all those emotions for? I must be realizing that I actually liked him too. That's it. Simple right? Well good, now we can possibly both be in attendance at Jason's future wedding and not be throwing daggers every time we look at each other. OK, this is good. *"Don't read more into this Tammy,"* I chided myself.

"Yah, sure I can go on later, you can let him know I'll be there." I wonder what he had to talk to me about. Oh well, I am sure I don't have to worry about it or think about it or him anymore today. After all, I had a lunch date tomorrow before work with a man that told me he loved me and that his clear intention with me and our relationship was marriage.

"K." Jason walked back down the hallway to let his dad know via email that I would be online tomorrow night. I would not see Jason again until tomorrow morning due to a new video game he purchased a couple of days ago. That left me with the dishes, probably a lengthy phone call to my sister and then a full nights rest on my agenda.

"Why would he think I was beautiful?" I mused to myself while washing the dishes. He definitely was still a charmer. Still a flirt, still playing with the emotions of women; flattering them with his play boy manner and softly spoken words. How does his girlfriend put up with it?

I remember the conversation we had online the other night. He was going in full detail about these two young, good looking girls that sat near him and his girlfriend at a restaurant a couple nights ago. He described to me so clearly their perfect little bodies and how their little waist and flat tummy's grew as they ate their meal. He never told me what his girlfriend ate, dressed like or talked about the whole time it was just about those two young women.

I am glad I am not with him anymore, I reminded myself. I would hate to be sitting across from the man that is supposed to be somewhat into me yet who was unable (or willing) to not keep his eyes or interest off of other girls. Poor girlfriend, it sounds like there is no interest in you anymore.

I gave the counter a quick wipe with the dish towel after the dishes were dried and put away, then turned to the task of phoning my sister. Settling myself on the end of the couch with a glass of juice and the cordless; I dialed her number.

"Hey what's up?" I spoke into the phone as soon as I heard her voice answer on the other end.

"What's up with you?" She responded. "I heard they were going to do a full scale restructure at work".

We worked for the same major health employer within the lower mainland BC. Although we were in different satellite offices we sometimes joined up when there was a need to be called out from our post to another area.

"I know I still want to go after an FTE of .74 if I can. It doesn't matter in what location although I would like it closer to the Mission". I responded

"I don't think I have the seniority to be picky and the higher ups are not letting anyone know anything yet as to where or when you are going to be able to bid on positions."

"Well, I wouldn't worry about it just yet." I told her with confidence. "They just had three major hires and that pushes you and I up on the scale. Plus, some of the older workers are planning on leaving and not bidding once it opens up."

"Alright, I won't worry. I have enough on my plate right now with my ex constantly on my ass about something."

"Why are you still putting up with the abuse? You are not married to him anymore; he has another wife now that he can treat like shit".

"I have to talk to him because of the kids."

I sighed deeply. She still allowed him to put her down and was constantly demanding his rights when it came to their two children.

"You know that it is possible for you to hang up on him when he starts being an idiot."

"Well then he just keeps phoning back. He won't stop until he gets his own way."

"Your kids are old enough now that they don't need mommy to be the go between." I commented.

"One day I will Tammy." As she said this we both knew that that one day was not in the near future.

"You do whatever you feel you need to do." I said.

"What about Mack. How is that going with Jason?" She changed the subject.

"It seems to be going good so far. No animosity between either party and Jason absolutely loves the fact that he has a 'dad' now."

"That is good for him." She said.

"Yah, it is good for him. He can finally talk about a dad when his peers talk about theirs."

"I think he may have hit some type of mid life crisis or something though. He seems to be very different from the man *or boy* I should say, that I knew a long time ago. He is a lot funnier than I remembered and appears to desire to have a relationship that is open and accepting with not only Jason but with me also."

"What do you mean?"

"Weeeeellll……" I paused for a while trying to think of what I did mean.

"Tammy….."

"Okay, like he is more interested in spending time online, which because of the distance is the only way he can spend time with Jason, but also with me."

"With you!" She had that 'tell me more' tone in her voice.

"Like right now, Jason is in his room playing a video game and talking to his dad on the computer."

"Okay, and with you….?" She wanted to hear more.

"I don't know yet. Or anything for that matter except that we have also been talking almost every night when I get of work."

"And….."

"And nothing. I am starting to enjoy talking to him and think it might be healthy for Jason to see that we can get along."

"Right. You still care about him".

I almost swallowed the phone. "WHAT! WHAT ARE YOU TALKING ABOUT! Absolutely not! He is in a relationship, I am in one and I would never even think of opening up that can of worms again!"

"Okay."

I hated the way she said that. I say it to her the same way. It is more like …."Okay, if you don't want to acknowledge reality, then we won't for now." It was that kind of "Okay."

"What do you mean …Okay. There is nothing more to it."

"Okay."

There was a silence. She told me that there was more to it by that silence.

"What are you thinking," I demanded.

"Tammy, every time you recount the conversations you have with him, you never tell me about his girlfriend. He obviously does not care about her and is probably just in his relationship with her still because he has not found any one else that he is willing to jump out of it for. A couple in love or in a long term relationship are always referring back to their other half. He never does."

"Maybe. But that has nothing to do with me. I don't care."

"How much time does he spend talking to you or Jason in a day?"

I had to think about that for a minute. "Around a couple hours a day."

"So, you are telling me that a man that has a life of his own, and that lives across the country from you will sit in front of his computer for a couple hours a day; not spending it with his girlfriend, to talk to you and or Jason, is not in love with you again."

The conversations and …yes…laughing that Mack and I had over endless subjects and many different forms such as shared jokes, puzzles, and day to day things or just straight talking, in the last couple months came flashing back to me. It hit me like a stone in the pit of my being. I looked forward to getting home and spending time with him online. He even phoned me a couple times and we must have talked for hours on those occasions also. The simple fact was that I lied to myself thinking that the only reason I was talking to him was because of Jason. The truth was that we did not need to talk to each other. The relationship that was supposed to have happened just between Jason and his dad was happening once again between Mack and I.

"Tammy," she interjected on my thoughts." Do you realize that you never talk about this guy you have been dating? All of our conversations when it comes to men are filled with 'what Mack said or did'."

I was still silent on the other end of the phone. My heart was beginning to cry out to God to stop what I knew was happening to it. 'Don't let me fall in love again with him' I begged, not again. It is over. It is imposable. It can't happen.

"You still there?"

"Yes." I didn't want to be on the phone anymore. Not that my sister was the cause of my sudden depression. It was more that I knew she was telling me the truth.

"Tammy....you still love him."

I lay in bed that night hating myself. 'Not again' I thought. It took me a long time to get over someone that I knew got over me, the moment he walked out my door. He was only thinking of his ski vacation and I was only thinking about him.

"GO TO SLEEP!" I commanded myself. Forget him.

Yet there was no way of doing that and instead, I not only thought of him until I fell asleep, I also dreamt about him that night. I woke up knowing that in order for me to end this I had to stop talking to him on the computer, responding to him via texts on my cell and definitely stop all other forms of communications such as the phone. Especially the phone. That is when I could hear his voice and the gentle manner in which he would talk to me and laugh with me and......be with me.

I had my lunch date and tried with everything in me to find the same type of interest that I had with this man before Mack came back into my life.

The lunch ended with the knowledge that I would not be able to love him like I did Mack but this must be where my future lays. Maybe I wasn't supposed to have a 'first love' feeling with the man I would marry at a mature age. Wasn't that feeling just for young, first time love? Then why was I feeling that now and not with the one I was supposed to feel it for.

This is crazy I thought. I would get busy thinking about marrying this other man and being with him and that alone is simply going to push Mack completely out of my mind! Done!

I went to work and did everything I could to not think about him. I stayed longer with patients talking to them about their lives and listening to their complaints or little stories. I tried to tell some jokes to those who I knew would like it. Then I met with a co-worker at A&W for supper.

It was no use. I don't know how, but I had fallen back in love with Mack. I couldn't keep him off my mind. He had 'sales man' charm and was experienced in using it, and he was 'selling' himself to me.

I needed to do something about this. So when I got home, I knew that I would have to let him know that I no longer could talk to him online. That I no longer could talk to him period. This had to end.

I got home just after my shift ended at around 11:15pm.

Jason came out of his room in the house coat that his dad left him when he left after their meeting in August.

"Two other kids dropped out of the AP biology class today. That only leaves four of us". He said.

He was such an amazing boy. I was proud of almost everything he did. He had such a grasp of science and numbers and was intelligent in so many other areas.

We only had a bit of time together during the week as I worked all evenings and he was in school during the day. He was planning on becoming a pathologist which would require becoming a Dr. first. Lots of schooling, but I knew he could do anything he put his mind to. He was so easy going and gentle in nature that I knew he would make an awesome Dr.

"So what does that mean for you?" I asked

He laughed, "More attention put on grading my papers."

We talked for a couple minutes before he retired to bed and I got ready to sit down at the computer for maybe the last time.

I changed out of my uniform and sat at the computer for a while before 'signing into msn' which was how we had been talking to one another.

How am I going to say it? I am sure he won't care and probably would find relief in not having to talk to me anymore. I don't want to be rude or mean.

'Jeepers, just sign in already! It is not like you are breaking up with the man!' I chided myself strongly and even chuckled at the thought of making this bigger than it was. 'He does not care about me.' I reminded myself. 'This is going to be easy. Just let him know that I am too busy for chit chat anymore….I wish him a happy life……glad he is in Jason's now……and talk to him at our son's futuristic wedding.'

I had it all figured out.

Then I signed in.

"Hello." I wrote

"Hello. How was your night?" was his response.

"Fine. Nothing new. It is starting to get a little colder." I lived in the Okanogan and had to rub it in. I knew he already was driving in snow and slush.

"My day was ok, but now it is better that I can talk to you."

I stared at the words for a moment. What does he mean? That I am the highlight of his whole day? That can't be. I tried to focus the subject in a different direction hopefully leading up to the end of us talking to each other.

"How is your girlfriend?" I asked

There was a pause, and then he startled me in what he responded with.

"I don't care, I am leaving her."

I was stunned.

"What do you mean! If your romance is going stale then take her out on a date! Go do something romantic."

"I don't want to."

"Have a candle lit dinner" I wrote.

"No."

This was not going very well and it definitely was not helping me stop our conversations. My fingers started to fly across the key pad without thinking out exactly what I was writing.

"I can't talk to you anymore."

"Why!"

The word came back at a surprisingly fast speed.

I sucked in some air as if I was running out of it and thought maybe the truth is better than any excuse I could think of. To be honest ….I really couldn't think of any other reason but the truth.

"Because I am starting to think about you way more than I should. Because I can't stop thinking of you even when I am with the man that has just asked me to marry him. Because I don't want to have feelings growing for anything that is not reality based."

There. I said it. Now he will have no other option than to back off. To let me go. This will scare him away for sure!

"So why don't you want to talk to me anymore?"

I read the sentence but was not sure if I had been clear enough in the 'why' department. I thought I just told him 'why'.

"I have to go now" I wrote."I am glad you have come into Jason's life. We might talk again one day."

There was no reply.

"Goodbye Mack."

There was still no reply.

I signed out.

3

Déjà vu

An unnatural fog covered the Okanogan in the early morning with a calm that seemed to force its inhabitants indoors. I started to laugh thinking how spoiled we were. If it is anything but vacation type weather, even during early winter, everyone seems to 'hide' until it is sunny. It never really takes long though. Even nasty weather passes quickly allowing all who live here to resume their activities as if nasty weather never happened.

There had been some historical disasters that forced us to realize we may live in a paradise setting, yet nature can deal harshly with us, just like the rest of the world. In those times Kelowna appeared to incorporate a small town atmosphere. We all came together to support our citizens that were dealt the hardest blows. Such as a couple major forest fires that took so many homes in different areas. I was definitely proud to have been born in this wonderful place.

It was Tuesday morning, my son was in school and I was doing some errands before I started work at three pm.

I had not talked to Mack for at least four days. I had not text him, emailed him or went on msn just in case he was online. My life was still full, yet somehow felt like there was something missing that made me feel not quite complete.

I was trying to clear my heart of these unsettling feelings of déjà vu. I knew now without excuses to myself that I still loved Mack just like I did during that summer a long time ago. It made me realize that maybe I had never really stopped loving him. I used to pride myself on knowing who I was and what I wanted in life. Always trying to put how I felt and what others needed together to do 'the right' thing by assessing facts not feelings. Now because of this new reality I felt like a tornado had just came through my world forcing me to rearrange the broken pieces it had left behind. Just like the fog, the knowledge of how I felt and accepting it settled around me unassisted and maybe, unwelcome.

As the day progressed the fog lifted and seemingly out of nowhere more and more people filled the streets with cars and sidewalks with pedestrians.

The sun was shining in all its glory by noon.

Finished in the bank (and all my errands for the day), I walked out into the wonderful sunshine. 'I need more sunshine,' I thought to myself.

I still had three hours before work, and didn't really want to leave this beautiful day to go sit in my condo.

As I settled into my car in the parking lot, before starting the engine I dialed my sister on my cell phone.

"What are you up to this morning?" I queried.

"Just finished repainting the living room wall and waiting for the paint to dry." She laughed. "What about you?"

"It's a wonderful day out. You want to try a game of tennis?"

"Ah I see something healthy. Will this be before or after we go for lunch?" We both knew 'lunch' would probably be something unhealthy. Although we did try every now and then to make our choice a sandwich shop or something along those lines, yet it usually fell on one of two choices.

"Okay, we will save tennis for our day off. Where do you want to meet? A&W or Arby's?"

"Arby's." She responded.

"Done. See you in about 15 then." I pushed the hang up button and started the car after we said goodbye and began thinking about what I was going to order before I got there.

Later that night as I drove home from work, pushing my way through traffic along with everyone else, I was a little ticked that the tourist season didn't seem to have ended. The roads were still full of cars and trucks hauling boats from the lake. At least the RVs have stopped I consoled myself.

Finally home, I pulled into my covered parking stall and turned off the engine. Before I could get out of the car I had to gather up my work bag stuffed with papers, medical gloves, hand sanitizer, children's chewable Tylenol (for me when I had a headache and no water for a real pill), pens, a safety belt for unstable clients and a change of shoes. The 'joy' of having your office on wheels meant having to clean it before leaving it.

Once I walked into the house and set everything down, my son came out to say hello and good night as par the course when I worked and we hadn't seen each other all day.

"Mom, I am talking to dad right now and he seems really upset."

"Okay, maybe not a 'hello how was your day then." I laughed. "What do you mean 'upset', did anything bad happen to him?" I took my jacket off hung it up in the closet by the door and placed my purse on the kitchen counter as I listened to him.

"No, but I am talking to him by texting because he said he was walking alone on Mount Royal and it must be around three in the morning there right?" He sounded concerned and was in around about way looking for some advice.

"Did he tell you why he was there?" Now I was a little concerned. Did something bad happen to him or his family?

"No." Jason looked puzzled. "He is only telling me that he is praying to God for something and he thinks his prayers are going unanswered."

Now I was puzzled, I didn't see Mack as a praying man. He claimed to be catholic but you didn't see any type of connection in him between actually having a relationship with Jesus and his understanding of what 'being a Christian' meant.

"Well what would you tell someone else that was looking to God for an answer to something?" I asked Jason this knowing that he would search himself and come up with a well thought out plan.

"I would tell someone that God say's to 'believe' that whatever we ask the father in the name of the Son, if it is to glorify God, then it will be done." Jason seemed satisfied with his own answer and with a mature nod of his head in my direction, he waited for my response.

"True, true and truer". I responded. "Try to find out what the problem is so we can both pray for him in regards to whatever the situation is that he needs prayer in."

Jason sat at the table and started texting with a speed in which makes me shake my head. This is the only thing that makes me feel 'not so young anymore', because when I text, it takes me a little longer than someone my son's age. Oh well, I know that I am not that old because my son says that all his friends think I am a 'hot mom'. I chuckled at that, but it pleased me to know that the wrinkles slowly appearing around my eyes and forehead must not be showing themselves clearly enough just yet. I hoped that my future husband would still find me attractive even after the wrinkles started to set in.

I sat at the table with him and reaching down started to untie my shoe laces when he began reading Mack's response from his cell phone.

"Mom," Jason hesitated, then said, "Dad just broke up with his girlfriend because he said he is in love with someone else. He said that his relationship was over with two years ago, he just never wanted to go through the hassle of actually separating everything. He said that the reason he is miserable is because he was in love with another woman and he is depressed at the thought that he may never be able to be with her."

Jason looked at me and suddenly there was an impossible thought that came over both of us almost at the same time. 'Why was he sharing this with us; unless it had something to do with us?'

Or, maybe it really has nothing what so ever to do with us but because he is just so torn up over this other woman he is in love with that he is just talking to anyone that will listen to him about it.

"Wow." I said. There was a sadness that entered my soul. How I wish he could have actually loved me like that when we first met. We could have raised Jason together and we.....'oh never mind Tammy.' I once again had to stop myself from drifting off to the 'what ifs'. 'You can't change anything with a wish.'

I watched as he began texting again with an easy, fast flow of fingers over his small key pad.

"I am telling him about trusting God for his heart's desire."

Jason looked as though he was texting more than what he had just told me he was, but I did not want to know more. I finished pushing my shoes off and went into my bedroom to change out of my uniform into some night cloths. When I was finished I just sat on the edge of the bed. The moon was so bright that it almost looked like there was a light on outside my bedroom window. Was it that bright for Mack on his walk right now? I stared at the closed door and then looked down at my queen sized bed.

Maybe I won't end up marrying anyone after all. Mack had my heart, I could not deny that and I didn't think it would be fair if I gave only part of me to another man. I sighed and looked up at the ceiling. "Maybe God, I was just never meant to get married until half my life is over. Maybe then maturity will finally kick in." I smiled as I said it in reference to my inability to lead myself in sound decisions without letting my heart get in the way.

There was a soft knock at my bedroom door. "Yes, come in." I answered.

The door opened and Jason said, "I told him we would pray for him and to believe he already had received from God what he wanted from Him." He came over and sat down beside me on the bed. "Mom, how was your day?"

I started laughing and pulled him into a big hug. "Everything went well my son, and how was your day?"

"Good. The school is doing this 'appreciate your school day' tomorrow and wants us to wear the school colors. Our colors are lame, so I don't think I'll participate." He paused, "I am going to wear my purple shirt instead." He said this with pure delight as if he had an Einstein moment.

"Of course Jason, that shirt looks great on you!" I leaned over and gave him a kiss on the cheek. "Then again," I offered, "everything looks good on you because you are such a good looking young man!"

"I know." He tilted his chin up in the air, gave me his cheesy grin and got up off the bed. "I am wonderful!"

"I mean it! I am not just a prejudiced mother talking here!" He was already walking out of the room as I threw that out to him.

"Good night mom." Jason was still smiling his cheeky smile at me as he left my room and disappeared out of site.

"Good night!" I said in a raised voice. "Have a good sleep and see you in the morning."

"Always." Came the reply from his bedroom.

I got up and went to the bedroom door to close it when I heard my cell phone announce with a ring that Jason programmed into it for me, that I had just received a text message. I never thought of who could be sending me one at this time because between my sister, brother or I, we would text or phone whenever we needed each other and always knew that the hour was never a problem. We never waited for a 'reasonable time'. When we needed someone to talk to, we would call, go visit or text right then. Sometimes it could just be because we were bored. I walked out of the room and went to my purse that was sitting on the kitchen counter where I had left it. I dug out my cell and opened it to read the new text. It wasn't from my sister or brother. It was from Mack.

"I can't stop thinking about you either."

My breath caught in my throat and I swear my heart wanted to jump out of my chest. I read the text again. What should I do? I read it again now holding the cell with a slight shake to my hands. Was it possible that this other woman was me? How should I respond?

'Think Tammy!' My mind was not co-operating with the rest of my body. I had to sit down and think. Turning to pull a chair out from the table, I struggled with disbelief. Still clutched the open cell phone in my hand as if I had no idea what it was for or how to work it, I sat slowly down.

The cell phone went off again.

"I love you."

Tears sprung up to my eyes as I stared at the words. Words that I felt I had been waiting to hear from him 18 long years ago. Years of struggling to be a whole family to my son, our son; even though it had just been me. Wishing he could appreciate the wonder of raising and knowing the awesome person his son is. Words that I thought I would never hear, and had so desperately wanted from him years ago.

"Now God?" I started to cry softly looking toward heaven. "After all this time.....he says it to me now?" The job of parenting that I would have needed him for is over. "What should I do?"

I felt love at that moment. That is what I needed to do. I needed to love him back. That is how I felt and I was not interested in playing any type of waiting game. I was going to let him know how I felt tonight.

I pushed the 'respond' button to his last text, and more slowly than I usually do; I typed the words that I had been feeling once again for him into the key pad. I examined them and the brief thought of 'should I' came and I quickly shoved it aside. Yes, I should. Then I pushed 'send'.

'I love you too…' left my phone with a quick 'message sent'.

No turning back now. I did it. I was in love with him again and just told him without being able to 'change my mind'.

I waited for what seemed like an eternity, then slowly closed the cell phone, got up and started walking back to my bedroom.

My home phone rang. I stopped and went to answer it knowing this time who it was. I knew it was not my sister……..or my brother. It was Mack.

4

Fast Track Dating

Jason and I were driving to the airport to pick Mack up. It was Jason's Christmas break from school and Mack was coming to BC to be with us for the whole week. We felt as excited as I am sure little people felt on Christmas morning.

The sun was shining on the snow that had fallen some time during the night, making everything appear like it was covered in a thin blanket made of diamonds.

This visit was going to be different. Mack and I had been spending every second we could spend together via the computer and telephone. When we were not near the computer or at home by our phones we would constantly be texting each other. We were both excited to be together again. Although I could not get any time off work, we were going to spend the time I was not working as a family. During my working hours it would just be Jason and Mack spending time together which was awesome. We had planned to do so many activities while he was down for the week.

Funny, I thought to myself how quickly things had changed. He told me his girlfriend had moved on and he was now living alone in an apartment above his parents place in Montreal.

Mack and I had spent many hours talking about how we would be together. I told him that I would not live with someone that I was not married to. I had done that once and would never do it again. So, we would have our own apartments but be in the same town so we could date and be together whenever we wanted to.

We began discussing a possible move to Calgary where we could all start a brand new life together. It was almost as if the 18 years of not talking to or seeing each other hadn't happened. Once again he was expressing his love and deep desire to be with me from across the country. Once again, I was holding my breath and doing everything I could to believe this time was the real thing.

He had grown up, I told myself. He now see's what is important in life and wants to enjoy it with his son…..and me.

I parked close to the exit doors of the airport, quickly got out of the car and walked with Jason towards the entrance doors. Once inside we checked the TV monitor to see if his plane had arrived.

"Well, we hurried for nothing." I commented.

Jason was reading the same thing I had. Mack's plane was going to be late. "Yah, you could have stopped at Timmy's for a coffee after all," he chuckled as he turned away from the TV and scanned the area for something to do while waiting. "Do you want to go up to the observing room? You can watch his plane land, it's not that exciting but better than doing nothing."

I nodded and we were on our way upstairs to a room with a wall sized window facing the runway. We therefore would have a clear view of all the planes arriving and landing.

Judging by the announced 20 minute expected delay; I knew that this was not going to be an exciting wait. Sitting across from us was an older man with a boy of about 10. That was it. No one else was in the room and nothing to read, except notices of air traffic conduct and commercial airline advertisements on the walls. This unfortunately gave me plenty of time to think.

What was I going to do when I seen him this time? Was I going to run into his arms for the first time after so many years had passed? Should I be more mature and wait for him to embrace me? Would he? How is he going to greet me this time now that we have expressed our renewed love for one another? What did I want to see happen? What did he want?

After going through several different scenarios, I settled on the one I liked most. I was going to go to him and embrace him. I wanted to be in his arms again. I didn't want to live by just words on a computer or spoken through the phone. I wanted it to be a reality. I needed to 'feel' his arms holding me and wanted to see if I could read real love in his eyes when he looked at me. I needed to 'touch' the love that I had up to this point only been hearing about.

I rested my head on the wall behind the chair and closed my eyes.

This love was meant to be, I told myself. It had to be didn't it? After all this time? All these years? It had to be.

My text message music when off on my phone as Jason announced there was a plane coming in to land. I looked up to see him standing in front of the huge windows watching it descend on the runway, as I reached into my purse for my cell.

It was a text from Mack. "I am landing," it read

The wait that had began to seem like forever now felt very short. My heart started increasing its pace as I got up from the chair I had been sitting in the whole time I was in the room.

No more daydreaming, this was real. I was going to see him.

"Mom, let's go." Jason was already walking to the stairs that led to the main floor after he watched the plane stop at its outside terminal.

I followed him trying to calm myself and stop this nervousness that wanted to take control of my emotions.

Jason saw his dad first and hurried towards him to help him find and pick up his bags.

I stopped. All of a sudden he looked wonderful to me. He gave Jason a hug, grabbed his bag and looking right into my eyes, started walking in my direction.

Stopping right in front of me, he placed his bag on the floor and embraced me. I tilted my head and raised myself to kiss him. The warmth of his arms around me and the tender kiss confirmed his love for me and mine for him. *This was real!*

We drove to my place so he could unpack. This time he was sitting in the front seat with me. He filled us in on how the flight went. That got everyone talking about planes and the different experiences that we all had on different trips. Jason was sitting comfortably in the back seat talking amiably about the times he had flown and how much he enjoyed it. I on the other hand only went in a plane when I had to. It was definitely not one of my favorite things to do.

Once back home, Mack, Jason and I ate lunch while we discussed what we wanted to do for the week.

One of those things Mack wanted to do, was go skiing. He wanted to ski in the Okanogan.

There was a slight uneasiness in me for a brief second but then I pushed it away. Things are different now. Jason had never skied downhill and this would be a good first time 'family' event for all of us.

Every second of our time was full of laughing, talking or just completely enjoying one another's company. We went to the mall, ate out several times visited my dad in Vernon and drove around the Okanogan being tourists. When I was working Jason and Mack did things together. After I got off work at 11 pm. I came home to spend my usual time talking to Jason before he went to bed, but this time instead of rushing to the computer to talk to Mack; I sat at the table or on the couch with him. We talked and laughed and shared stories till we were both too tired to talk anymore.

I had two days off at the end of the week that he was down visiting us in. I was sad at the thought that he would have to leave soon and we would be back talking on the computer or phone. Yet, I forced myself to 'be in the moment'. I wouldn't think about him leaving until he was actually gone.

The day before I had to drive him to the airport we went skiing.

It put a mar on my little dream world and I wasn't sure how to deal with it.

Everything seemed to be going well. Mack rented the skis for us and after walking/sliding around the ski rental station for 15 minutes, we set off to stand in the lineup for the ski lift.

"Mack, Jason has never skied downhill before. I don't know if taking him up to the top is the best idea." The protective mother bear in me was concerned for her son!

"It will be fine Tammy; this is the best way for him to learn." I could see that Mack was not open to discussing this. He made up his mind and I could see it in his eyes. I was a little unsettled by this turn in him. I started getting the feeling that he was doing this purely for his own pleasure and not to enjoy a family outing.

This is nonsense, I scolded myself. *Don't read into things and just enjoy the day.*

I asked Jason if he was okay with this and he shrugged half heartedly. "Mom if this is what dad wants I will try to do my best."

I watched Jason as he awkwardly, for the first time ever, managed to catch the chair on the lift and hold his poles so they would not fall. Mack and I quickly sat in it with him at the same time. Jason was really trying to do what he thought his dad wanted him to do. He really wanted his dads love and friendship. My heart went out to him and saying a quick prayer, I hoped that I was doing the right thing and that Mack would not hurt his son in anyway. I prayed silently and thought, *don't judge Jason Mack, just love him like he loves you!*

We got to the top and slid off. Jason almost fell but caught himself in time. I could see a determination on his face to prove that he could do this.

I stood beside Jason at the top of the mountain. We looked out over the valley and took the view in.

"It is beautiful up here." I commented.

"Yah," Jason returned. "I can see why people would get hooked on this sport."

"You know how to start?" I asked trying desperately not to show my concern for him as much as I could see that he was hiding his dislike for the sport already. He did not want to be in this position. I could see that in his face even though there was very little emotion showing on him. I could see it.

Jason glanced at his dad who was looking at the other skiers getting off the lift and quickly pushing themselves away from it to start their decent. He looked back at me.

"You can put your skis in a V shape to start going slowly. You don't want to just point them straight down Jason or you will get too much speed and lose control. You turn using your body pushing down on the ski that you want to turn away from." I showed him what I meant by leaning on my right leg pushing down on the ski and motioning with my arms that I was going to go to the left.

He put his skis in the V shape.

"Bring them slowly open at the end to get some speed in that direction, then again to a V and slowly lean and push down on the other leg which should start swinging you back to the right."

"Come on lets go." Mack stood beside us not able to hide his eagerness to ski any longer.

"Why don't you go and we will follow slowly." I could feel myself getting upset for bringing my son up here. He couldn't even pretend to have any patients with a new skier, even if the new skier was his son.

"No, I'll stay with you." Mack wanted to ski, not 'stay with us', he was not hiding that at all very well.

Jason saw it too. You could read a hurt appear in his eyes that said he was going to push himself to not disappoint his dad. My heart sank. I saw Jason determine right there that he was going to have to 'earn' his dad's love. He pushed himself and slowly started to descend the mountain.

"Come on mom!"

"Right behind you kiddo." I wanted to be in front of him in case he started going too fast, but accepted trailing behind him. He was going down slow, but he was doing it! I felt like I was watching him walk for the first time and chuckled that I would never tell him that or he would get upset and remind me of his age.

Half way down and it had become too much. Jason was doing great for a first timer and had only fallen twice. Mack though, was now not hiding that he wanted to go on his own and ski but didn't want to make this look like this trip was for his pleasure. He wanted to keep up the guise of this trip being for the 'family'.

This had not been a good idea. You don't just throw someone at the top of a mountain with skis on and say..."Now let's have fun!" You show them some technique first. You know…how to stop, turn and speed up…stuff like that. It was strange that I felt I had to tell him to go do what I saw he desired to do.

"Mack go ski. Jason and I will make our way down slowly and meet you at the bottom."

Mack said ..."Okay, then I'll just do a couple runs," and he took off down the hill.

Why did we have to go to the 'very' top? Jason was now no longer hiding the fact that this trip had solidly confirmed within him, that he had no desire to become a skier.

"This is going to take all night just to get down the hill." He complained. "Mom, I hate to disappoint you, but I don't like skiing downhill. I like cross country skiing only."

"What is wrong with that?" I asked him. "Nothing!" I answered for him. "It is still a long way down, let's try to make this fun and after we get to the bottom, you will never have to do this again!"

"Great! I won't!"

After falling and laughing and face planting in the snow a couple dozen times we made it down the hill. Mack was nowhere to be seen so we decided to practice on a smaller slope outside the ski rental shop.

It was dark and snowing lightly. The place was decorated for Christmas with millions of little lights everywhere and we were having fun. We moved to the bunny hill and Jason was going down as fast as I was after several trips.

"What do you think Jason? Have you changed your mind about downhill skiing now that you are so good at it?" I was smiling at the funny expression he had on his face.

"Are you kidding me? Never! I won't give up cross country for this!" He was laughing with me as we once again walked clumsily back to the shop to check and see if Mack was there yet. We had been checking for him after ever short run down the bunny hill, before we went for another one.

He was there drinking an espresso. The evening was over. It was time to go home.

We took our skis off and gave them back to the young woman that had rented them to us. I was sure that Jason promised himself never to touch them again as he placed them on the counter by the way he looked down at them. I had to laugh at that. I made a mental note to ask him if he thought that later.

"Did you have fun?" I asked Mack.

He went into complete detail about the runs he went on and started talking about the difference in this mountain and the one he went to in the States. As he was talking he also mentioned that he would not bring us skiing again. To us, as Mack said this, it sounded like it was more on the lines of 'it was a waste of money to have brought us' rather than 'I realize you don't enjoy skiing'.

At that point I could see Jason slow his pace. He never said anything.

How could he have just said that? It is 'OKAY' to not enjoy or be good at something! AND.....whether he was good or bad at something ...Jason is ALWAYS worth the money! I started to get mad at him for the hurt that I saw in my sons face.

"You were awesome!" I told him quietly.

He looked at me for a second without responding, then with a sudden grin, looking me in the eyes proclaimed...."I know completely awesome!"

Now we were both smiling as we walked through the snow at least 7 feet now behind Mack. He never turned around to see if we were even still with him. Jason and I just followed behind him, watching him walk to the parking lot.

As we passed some people that were outside drinking, I couldn't help but notice that Mack seemed to be turning slightly and walking directly toward a young, drunk, blond woman that was not doing a great job at holding her balance. On a path that was about 25 feet wide with no one in our way; he started walking directly to her. He never took his eyes off of her. You could see their gaze locked together for his approach up to and pass her. Only to be broken once he had completely passed her, and his shoulder brushed against her arm, almost making her spill her drink.

I saw Jason turn his head in my direction, so I looked at him. He didn't say anything as we walked past the same girl that was still staring at Mack's departing figure. Only unlike Mack, we had about 8 feet between us and her.

"I didn't just see that." I said to Jason as we neared the vehicle that Mack was now at and had finally turned to see if we were still even with him.

There was a deep sigh that came from Jason. "No, I guess I never either."

Just before we got close to the vehicle and within Mack's hearing, I asked Jason a question that almost needed no answer.

"Mack did just ask me to marry him today right? He *wants'* to be with me…right?"

I needed to confirm this with someone because what I just seen looked to me like a single man that was impressed with someone else and wanted them to know it. A single man that was not walking with any other woman. You could not guess at that moment that we were together; he was way too far ahead of Jason and I.

"Yah mom, that's what he said he wanted," was my son's reply.

5

Telephone Cross Messages

"The young woman leading the biking class had huge boobs."

"Really?" My mind stopped enjoying the conversation with Mack instantly.

"Her waist was so small and…."

"You mean as small as the young girl that you told me about the other day that was wearing a small chain around her waist?" Didn't he start this conversation off with an…"I miss you so much and need to be with you, type speech?" Why did it seem like the conversation always had something to do with another woman in it? Always another '*young*' woman in it.

"Yes Tammy, every guy in the place were staring at her, some even stopped in a game of racquetball to watch her walk pass the window."

Hmm, I thought to myself, sometimes it wasn't just his English that sounded a little off. Apparently he couldn't keep his eyes off of her either or he wouldn't have noticed everything she did, everywhere she went and the reaction she was getting from everyone else.

"Her boobs were almost too big for her small body". He laughed at himself, probably keeping the image of this amazing creature in his mind. He was laughing alone, because I was not laughing with him.

"Maybe you should ask her out on a date." I couldn't believe he felt it necessary to tell me about other woman. If he was so smitten with this girl, than he should rethink his desire to marry me hence moving himself back into the dating scene.

"What are you talking about?" I could hear a light tinge of annoyance in his voice. "I was thinking of you the whole time I was looking at her. I knew I must be in love with you when I was looking at her. "He kept going, "This is a compliment to you!"

Wow! I was sooo missing the compliment in this. I was soooo missing all the compliments he seemed to like to give me by letting me know about all the young women he seen, noticed, smelled or talked to. "Mack, you don't think of one woman while admiring the boobs of another. That is not a compliment.

There was a pause on the other end of the phone.

It had been almost two months since we seen one another. He had gone back to Montréal and I had given my notice of resignation at work. It was a 4 month notice; my employer had plenty of time to replace me. I was quitting to get married and move to Montréal. Mack backed out of our move to Calgary and said that the job position that he wanted was not ready yet, so we would have to live in Montréal for a couple months until one opened in Calgary for him. He assured me that it would be no problem for me to get a job in Montréal and it wouldn't be for long anyway. So, our plans were…I give up my job, family, friends and car; to move and be with him. It would only be for a couple months he told me.

Jason thought it would be an adventure for us. He was looking forward to meeting new people and being a family……he was looking forward to being with his dad. He was even looking forward to starting his college years in Montréal and felt it would not be too much bother to get transferred to Calgary when the time would come for the move there.

"If you don't get it that is your problem!" Mack was annoyed now.

"Maybe I should let you go now, have a good day Mack." This conversation was making me feel unsure of our pending marriage. I needed to be off the phone with him.

"I love you Tammy." His voice changed; there was urgency in it. "I can't wait to be with you and Jason. I can't wait for you to be here."

"Are you sure this is what you want?" I knew that I loved him, but sometimes I got the feeling that maybe we should not get married right away. I could get an apartment there and we could date each other in Montréal before getting married.

"I can't wait for you to be here, I need you." His voice softening into what appeared to be genuine tenderness for me, transformed the conversations direction. "This is all I want. I can't wait for you to meet my friends. This week I went to a comedy show with a friend from my work out class and we had such a good time. She wanted to know that you were not a jealous type because she wants to keep doing things with me and having a relationship with me."

"She wants to KEEP the relationship with you that she has now, even after you are married to someone else?" I was starting to get a headache now trying to believe he really loved and wanted me. "Why don't you date her?" Now I really wanted off the phone.

I was tired of hearing about all these other women in his life. I remembered another conversation we had not too long ago about his neighbor's daughter. He was so very excited about Jason and I meeting this young 17 year old girl. She lived in the other half of the condo with her parents. The condo in which his parents owned one side of and this girl's parents owned the other. He was living in the suite above his mom and dad, of course on their side. The suite as he informed me, that Jason and I would also be living in when we would make our move to Montréal.

He told me several times how much she had a huge crush on him and even sent me a picture of the two of them sitting very close to each other in a hot tub (with his mom on the other side of the picture), just to show me how "incredible" her body looked in a new bikini she had bought. He said that when she found out that Mack was going to be in the hot tub, she pretty much raced to her room to put it on and show him. To be with him in the hot tub.

"Tammy, because I love you." The conversation continued.

"Mack, I am not going to marry a man that thinks he can keep doing things with other women. You need to know this now. If you want to keep enjoying other women like you apparently do, then I am not the woman for you."

"I don't want anyone else! I want you!"

I remembered his account of when he went on a snow shoeing event one evening with this same wonderful woman and his parents. 'It was such a romantic night,' he would tell me later via an msn conversation between the two of us.

"Then end your relationship with this woman now, before I move there. I am not going to be sitting at home while you go off to a function with another woman." I was getting sick and tired of hearing about other women! I needed to get off the phone with him. The mixed messages I was getting constantly from him were messing me up.

"You would like her when you meet her." He stated quite pleased with himself at the thought.

I didn't respond to that one. Yah, I can see it now….."hey how's it going? You want my husband tonight? No problem, just drop him off when your through with him." Not likely, I thought. Was it not registering with him that I am not impressed with all the girls that want him??? I DIDN'T CARE!

48

"I can't wait for you to be here, to be with me." His voice got very quiet and gentle. "I love you so much Tammy."

"I know," I sighed as I heard him confess his undying love for me once again. "I have to go now. I will talk to you later Mack."

"I love you and miss you so much Tammy." It sounded like he was pouring out his heart to me.

"I love you too Mack." We hung up the phone after saying goodbye.

I moved to the couch and sat down; almost numb now from trying to sort out all the mixed messages I sometimes got from him.

Am I going to marry a man that believes he doesn't need to be satisfied with just one woman in his life? I thought when you get married you have a 'best friend' that you now plan things with. Do I really want to go out for an evening with him and another woman that I know wants a relationship with him? Wouldn't that be like, me still wanting to do things with a man that I know wants to sleep with and have a relationship with me? The only difference of course after I was married would be that I would bring my husband with me on our 'dates'.

My mind was not okay with this and I didn't know why he would expect me to be okay with this?

No. I made up my mind. I am more than willing to give up other men in my life that are interested in me for more than just friendship, and I will expect the same from him. I believe that once you are married you no longer encourage the opposite sex into thinking that they still have a chance with you. Truly I felt he should not marry me if he wants to have more time being single and enjoying the company of these other woman. I wanted to marry a man that wanted to spend his life with just one woman. I would let him know how I felt the next time we talked. I wanted to give him a wide open door to live free until he finds a woman that will actually satisfy him enough to want to be married and give up a single man's lifestyle. A married person should have friends, but only look to their spouse for comfort, intimacy and secret sharing.

It was now almost 25 minutes past midnight and I wanted the peace that I hoped would come from sleep. Jason was over at a friends' for the night so I had the place to myself. I walked around and made sure the doors were locked, lights were off and went into my bedroom to change out of my uniform that I still had on. As soon as I had walked into the house after work, the phone was ringing and it was Mack, so I never had time to change.

After getting into a t-shirt that I usually slept in, I walked down the hall to the washroom without a housecoat. I was home alone, I could do that, I smiled at my freedom.

I hardly ever wore make-up, so I had none to take off and washing my face took a minute. Brushing and flossing my teeth took longer.

I paused from the task of flossing as I looked at myself in the mirror. *You deserve someone that loves you and wants to be with you!* I told my reflection.

I was more than ready to be faithful and honest to one man. I could picture him and I going on vacations together and enjoying life. Going out to live theatre and talking about it afterwards. Sharing our lives with each other and enjoying the company of friends and family that supported our union.

Yes, being married to someone that 'wanted' to be off the market, and wanted to be faithful to that union was very important to me. I did not want to get some sexually transmitted disease or live in a triangular relationship with another woman. I would be honest, committed and faithful to him. If he was not able or willing to give this back then it would not work. He would need to find a woman that was okay with sharing her mans affections.

I finished flossing and brushing my teeth, shut off the washroom light, walked down the hall into my bedroom to sink comfortably into my bed.

Sleep was more than welcome, and it came to give me a wonderful full nights rest.

Sitting at a table listening to my brother tell some funny stories about his job was interrupted by the phone ringing. No one moved to get it. My dad was laughing too. His presence made everything seem right. The phone was still ringing. My nieces and nephews were running around the house. The phone rang without stopping. I turned to ask someone to answer it and smacked my hand against my bedside night table.

Slowly my eyes opened and sleep started to leave my body. The phone rang again.

It's my phone!

I threw the covers off my body and jumped out of bed. Scrambling hastily to the living room where the phone was still ringing. *How long was it ringing before it woke me from my sleep?*

"Hello?" I asked in a groggy voice.

"Good morning my love." Mack sounded much too awake. What time was it, I wondered. I glanced at the time displayed on the VCR; it read 8:30a.m.

"Good morning." I answered.

"I have great news for you!" He sounded very happy about something. "My friend is going to buy my ex girlfriends part of our boat!"

Way too early for this. What time was it there? When did he get this information? What time did his friend get up? I must be missing something here. My mind was still waking up. I held the cordless phone and walked into the kitchen to start making myself a cup of coffee.

"Are you saying he is going to buy her out?" Mack and his ex girlfriend owned a sailboat together which tied them and their bank account together for as long as they were both owners of this thing.

"Yes, we are going to the bank today to sign the paper work."

"I hope everything goes well for you." I was watching the coffee slowly start to come out of the machine and fall creating a dark pool of liquid at the bottom of the pot.

"Are you working tonight?" He enquired. "When can I call you and tell you how it went?"

Opening the cupboard for a large coffee mug, I mentally went over my work schedule. "No, I have today and tomorrow off."

"Okay, I will phone you tonight then." He sounded excited about the prospect of owning the boat with his friend rather than his ex.

The sailboat. That was another one of those strange calls I had from him that sent me to bed confused and wondering if we should actually be getting married.

"Alright, have a good day and talk to you tonight then."

"Good bye my love." His voice was soft and reassuring.

"Good bye Mack."

"I love you…"

"I love you too Mack." I really did. I felt like he was doing everything he could in that moment to make sure we would be happy together and have our own life. I felt warm and in love.

We hung the phone up and I thanked God for this change of events.

I remember how confused I was over one of our 'boat talks'. I felt unloved by him and totally misunderstood. I felt like I could not communicate properly, making up a fight between the two of us where there should not have been one.

We had been talking about the boat. A boat he planned on taking Jason and I on.

"She doesn't want you to go on the boat." He had said it with an unmistakable authority in his voice.

"Okay, we just won't go on the boat together than." I responded.

"She has a right to say that, it is still half her boat!" Now he sounded angry with me.

"Okay Mack, I understand how she would feel that way. We can do other things; I don't need to go on the boat. I don't even know how to sail anyway." I tried to let him know that this was not a problem for me.

"If she wants to say who goes on or not it is her right."

I looked at Jason as he was sitting across from me at the kitchen table when Mack and I were having this conversation through the computers' msn. My look was total confusion. He had been repeating himself for almost three hours and I was getting upset now myself. My look said to Jason 'am I not agreeing and telling him that I will respect her wishes? Jason shook his head a little like....'yah I don't get it either.'

"Mack! I am telling you that I can completely see her side to this! If I was in her shoes and my ex boyfriend and I owned a camper together that we dreamed about retiring in and worked hard on; than I would not want to have him taking another woman out camping in it!" I felt like I was going in circles here.

"You just have to live with the fact that we own the boat together and she can say who goes on or not!" He was angry with me and I no longer knew how to tell him that I was not fighting him or her on this issue.

He kept the circle of argument going for another three hours. Every time I wanted to sign out of msn because I felt like I was the bad person here trying to create this fight with him, he would not let me go.

I tried every way in which my language allowed me to portray that I did not want to tell her or him what to do in regards to the boat. I agreed to not go anywhere near the boat and had no hard feelings about how she felt.

He continued to defend her, putting me down a couple of times. I didn't understand what was making me the bad guy in this and why was he defending her against me when I was almost telling him that I was on her side in this matter.

This was not the first upsetting conversation we have had about the boat. My mind snapped to attention on this subject and I decided I now actually hated 'the sail boat'.

When he started to verbally put me down, I started to cry and signed out.

I sat at the table and cried. I didn't understand what that was all about. Jason came over to me and gave me a hug.

"That was crazy mom." He kissed my forehead and just held me.

"Why did he leave her if he still has so much respect and love for her?" I really and truly did not see how I started that argument. Whenever he mentioned the boat to me before this conversation it was only to talk about plans of sailing with me. I felt like he never heard anything I said to him. It was like I wasn't even part of the conversation. That he was just mad at this unrealistic person (me) and had to lecture me about his ex girlfriends rights. He made it quite clear that I was to respect them as much as he does.

The funny (not laughing funny) thing about it all was that *I was respecting her wishes!*

The phone rang and Jason let go of me to answer it. It was Mack. Jason hesitated before giving me the phone.

"I am so sorry." He said. "I didn't mean to make you cry!"

"Okay." I didn't know what to say and hadn't had time to settle my upset heart down.

"I don't know why I do that," he went on, "I make my sister and mom cry too."

I didn't respond. I didn't know what to say, although I had stopped crying.

"I don't want to make the woman I love cry."

The way he said that burned itself into my memory. I don't know why. I think something told me that I needed to remember these very statements from him.

"It's ok," I told him. "I understand you must be under a lot of stress right now."

"I love you Tammy so much."

"I love you too Mack, but I won't have a conversation like that again with you." This was not the first strange conversation I had with him pertaining to the boat. Yet now, I was going to definitely make it the last one!

"As long as you own the boat with her, I will not be involved with it ......or you." I couldn't believe I was saying this to him. I couldn't believe I would throw my relationship with him away over a stupid boat. But, it wasn't the boat. It was more the fact that he was standing up for someone else and made me feel like a piece of garbage. It was the fact that MY husband was supposed to stand up for me. Not another woman.

"You decide what you want Mack, go after it and be happy." Tears filled my eyes again. "I am going to say goodbye to you and you should think about getting back together with her so the two of you can keep your boat."

I hung up the phone. I was not mad. I made that statement in a soft low tone. I was not going to get scolded over that boat again.

Now though, after this early phone call today, from Mack about the boat it looked like the boat issues would be finally over. After today, the other half of the boat will be owned by his friend. I breathed a deep sigh of relief. I hoped that now we could have 'normal' conversations without suppressed anger from him over 'the boat'.

6

Ending Single Life

No one would have thought that time would go so quickly. My dad was already having a hard time with the fact that I would be a married woman and then gone to live so far away from him. The wedding and move itself will be over in less than two weeks. After a short 'honey moon' that will include all the time spent with his mom, dad, sister and friends, we would be riding in a U-Haul across Canada. My sister and I were trying to get as much 'sister time' in with each other as we could before my departure. My brother was planning his own move from the Okanogan to go further up north with the woman he loved, so we were seeing each other more too. My son also was doing all he could to spend more time with his friends. They had enjoyed their graduation ceremony and now had free time to do whatever they wanted, which seemed to be Barbequing at one another's houses.

Mack had come and gone with the aid of Jason not cashing one of his child support checks from his dad to pay for his flight. With the visit were the promises. I would give up my car and get another one in Quebec. I would get a job right away because the province needed health care workers very badly. It won't be for long until the job for Mack opened up in Calgary and we would move there together. Jason was going to love the college there and Mack had already started to line up a couple young girls for him to meet, such as daughters of co-workers and the young neighbor that had a crush on Mack. To which Jason had asked me to talk to his dad and tell him that he was quite capable of meeting his own friends once he gets there. Of course Jason asked me to be nice about it but he was uncomfortable with the thought of someone trying to match make him especially his dad. He really didn't like the thought of Mack appearing so intent on introducing him to girls.

Mack's family and a couple of his friends would come down with him for the wedding of which I tried to make a small affair. After all, neither Mack nor I seemed to desire a large ceremony. I was just so happy that my dad was well enough to walk me down the aisle. That meant a lot to me, as I am sure it does to all girls that adore their dad. The wedding after everything was paid for and rented cost me under 4 thousand dollars. I could see how they could be so much money because when everything was said and done you honestly could not see where it had gone, or I couldn't anyway.

I only had two more days left of work and then I would be unemployed, but not for long I would tell myself. I would get a job right away after a little time adjusting to married life and the transition from BC to Quebec. I would give myself a month I thought.

The trees were in full bloom and looked like a fairy tale story book when you drove down certain streets.

With my car's speed at around 30 kilometers, I was winding my way up a hill in the old part of Kelowna that still boasted of beautiful large orchards to get to a clients' house. It was around 5:30 p.m. and yet looked and felt like noon with the sun still shining down warmth in its golden rays.

I finally reached the address I needed and pulled into the driveway. Shutting off the ignition, grabbing my work bag and spare pair of shoes, I got out of the car and started for the door.

I didn't have to ring the bell this time for the dear woman was waiting for me with the door open.

"Hello Tammy, I am happy to see you but sad this will be our last visit." She smiled at me as she always did but today there was a little sadness at the edge of her eyes. Her frail voice seemed to echo this feeling of loss.

I gave her a hug at the door.

"Hello back. I came a little early to see you so we could spend a bit more time together. I know you will be fine without me though Kelly, all of my co-workers love you and enjoy your company."

After walking into her home and changing my shoes I reached for her medical service plan and started dialing a code into my cell phone. She was moving slowly around her kitchen pouring herself a cup of tea and looking at me silently motioning to ask if I would want one.

"No thank you." I smiled in reply and started placing my initials where they needed to be, finished with the cell phone and set these things aside to get supplies I needed out of my bag.

"How much longer until the wedding dear, I think you said it was the end of this month right?" She sat down with her tea beside me at the table and gently placed her leg on a stool between the two of us.

"Five more days from today, and trust me, I am glad I decided to work until three days before the wedding or I would probably be too nervous to go through with it." Putting my gloves on and using some saline I slowly started to peel back the old Adaptec sticking to her lower leg.

She watched me intently and sipped at her tea.

"I wish you all the joys possible Tammy. May your marriage be a happy one, you deserve it."

"You need more bactroban girl, and thank you so much for those wishes!"I started to pat her leg around the almost closed wound with gauze to dry the small drops of saline I used to loosen and remove the old bandaging. "I shall take all the well wishes I can get. It is going to be a big move and a different type of world for me. "I looked up into her beautiful grayish brown eyes. "Have you ever made a big move like this Kelly?"

"Oh dear me yes." She straightened up and drew a large breath in before going on, as if to illustrate just how huge of a move she was remembering. "Why I began my life here in Canada as a young war bride. And I tell you, it took me a year worth of waiting for a ship and all the red tape to be cut before I landed on this dirt. And a pile of dirt it was too!" She rolled her eyes up to heaven. "He was a farmer living in the middle of nowhere! Why my dear Tammy, I think I cried longer than it took me to get here for a driving wish to go back home! All my dreams of what I was walking into where all but gone as I stepped off the train and into my new husband's auto. He was charming enough and more than glad to see me….."she paused here…. "I think I was as happy but the trip to get to him was so long and tiring, that maybe because of that it was that I didn't show him as much back."

Kelly paused again and her small thin hand wiped at her forehead as if it would erase a bad memory.

"Yes, I thought I was going to go crazy with the isolation that I felt on that farm. I would cry myself to sleep almost every night and pray that God would allow me to go home to my family. One morning almost a year after I got there, I packed my bags and started to walk out to the main road. I knew one of those greyhound buses passed by and would pick people up to take them somewhere else". She started to chuckle at this point and shook her head as if the moment she was retelling was happening now. She looked down at her freshly wrapped leg and leaned back in her chair to look at me as I was replacing the last item of mine back in my bag.

"You are finished then, do you have to run?"

"Heavens no Kelly, I want to hear more of your story!" I closed my work bag and sat more comfortably in the chair at the table to gladly give Kelly my full attention.

She smiled and I thought I could see a joyful gleam come into her face as she relaxed and with a satisfied nod, continued her story.

"You know, I think I packed too much in my suitcase that day because as I walked it seemed to get heavier and heavier. Several times I had to set it down and sit on it for a rest. At those times, I would think about maybe taking something out to lighten it yet knew if I took anything out I would surly miss the item once I had gotten to my home country." She laughed again, "besides; what would my husband have thought when he came home from town and had to pick up my clothes all along the driveway?"

Kelly was still smiling at that thought as she attempted to take another sip of tea out of a now empty cup. Instantly she took it away from her mouth and looked into it with a frown as if it was the cups fault for not having any more earl grey tea in it. "Tsk"! She said softly and put the cup down on the table as though reprimanding it.

I smiled and completely enjoyed watching her animation. She was such a joy to listen to. It always amazed me that such a woman as Kelly, that for the most part you felt you wanted to hug and protect from the world; could survive and thrive through all the things life had thrown at her.

She never allowed herself more than one cup of tea after she ate her dinner around five because she felt this would make her get up at night to go to the washroom too many times. Yet, she always appeared disappointed when her tea cup was empty, almost like the cup dribbled it out while she was not looking, therefore denying her one last sip.

She shrugged and looked back towards me. "I never knew exactly how long of a walk it would be to get to the main road. I think I walked almost to dinner time, I was hungry and it was starting to get a little dark and chilly with the sun hiding behind the trees. So, I finally gave up. I sat my case down and rested on it trying to think of what to do. I was now too tired to walk forward or back for that matter. So, sitting on my suitcase I prayed to Jesus that if he would send me an auto going either way I would take the ride. And where the LORD wanted me to be in His divine decision He would send an auto going in that direction." She raised her hand as if in surrender to heaven and smiled again looking me right in the eye. "Would you know that the next auto that came down the road after waiting for just five minutes of saying that prayer.......was my husband coming home from town?"

Driving home in the dark, once work was over and I had dropped of my finished work schedule at the satellite office mail box; I reflected on all the wonderful clients I so enjoyed to see. I hope I don't forget any of the stories I had listened to. Or forget the people that had passed on, yet allowed me to love them through sharing so much of their lives ups and downs with me.

I was going to miss so many of them. I absolutely loved several of the men and women that would share their real life stories with me. I would think sometimes about what I would do in their cases. Would I be as strong? As a single mother I definitely had times of hardship but looking back I really had very few regrets. I loved my son immensely, was very proud of him and thought that what I had gone through in life to get where I am had molded me into the woman I am today. God still had a lot of work to do in me, but I will have no regrets over the changes in me He has already done.

I will be married soon.

I only have tomorrow to work in this job. Then I hand in my identification and that is it.

My son is working hard on putting music together for the wedding and excited about lighting the candles for his dad and I during the meal at the rented Hall. After of course the marriage ceremony at the church. Even though he knows he is going to miss his friends he is very excited about another new adventure in his life. He is excited about having his dad in his life.

The darkness seemed to thicken as I drove through Kelowna back to my condo. Jason would not be there tonight. He is at his friend's house for a going away BBQ and movie night.

I sat at a red light waiting for it to change. Everything seemed so quiet. The night seemed to take on an unreal sense about it, or maybe it was just my thoughts rolling the idea around of me marrying a man I thought I had loved then hated and now loved again. I am going to marry my son's dad. I can enjoy the freedom of living in forgiveness and the freedom of forgiving so I know once again how to live in love.

The light turned green and I slowly made the turn in the now almost deserted streets for home. Driving down Gordon towards my home, I realized that I was definitely going to miss so much, and so many. I wrote a letter to my co-workers last week. I don't think they knew how much they have impacted my life. I had to let them know.

The letter read.....

A Special Moment

You know when sometimes you have a moment in time that touches your heart and you just feel like sharing it with others....well I had one I want to share with you.

I had purchased the wrong sized florescent light bulbs and was a little flustered at having to go back to Rona to exchange them. Dragging the old one with me so I would not make that mistake twice and balancing the wrong sized ones praying that they would not break; I walked carefully into the store. Thoughts of my "to do list" played tag with each other in my head. While the sinking knowledge that no matter how many tasks I seem to be running around and doing, did sadly not seem to lessen my list. Will I make it in time? Will I get everything done I need to do? Can I do everything myself? My mind full, I was only half aware of the lady behind the counter helping me with my exchange. Then...resigning myself to one more chore, I hurried down the aisle to find the right item and the right sized ones at that.

Then, I walked quickly past a co-worker, whom appeared to be in a bit of a rush also. We smiled at each other, nodded our heads in a simple greeting but both kept walking. My task was done and paid for and I was just about to pick everything up from the counter and walk out when I felt a gentle hand touch my arm. I looked up and was greeted with a beautiful smile. It was my co-worker. She paused long enough to say hello again and wish me a good day. She laughed and said a comment about working hard that made me laugh too. Then....she was out the door while I was still gathering my awkward bundle.

I looked for her as I left the store but she was gone. Then....it struck me. My pace slowed down and my heart felt heavy. I could have begun crying right there walking to my car in the parking lot of Rona. Now that would have been a scene, but I didn't care.

All of a sudden other thoughts filled my head erasing for a moment my long 'to do list'.

Flashes of memories came to mind. Memories as simple as walking in a grocery store and bumping into a co-worker, friend or family member. Stopping to talk about the weather, husbands/boyfriends, tourists that are now and will yet be plunging into Kelowna and clogging up our main roadways. Talk of fighting traffic as more and more trucks with campers or boats make their way to this destination or that. Getting advice on kids and sharing achievements. Or just having someone to vent to about a life struggle, be it small or large. Memories of waving to someone you know as you drive up to a service station or getting encouragement from others in your moments of darkness. Smiling with others and laughing over moments of joy. Simply put....wherever I go....there is a smile I know I may bump into....somewhere....to make my day brighter.

The wonderful smile I received today in Rona was both uplifting and yet sad. I won't be able to tell her how her smile made my morning bright. But I can take this time to let you all know how I love going to work because of you all. How no matter what is taking place in the hours before work I know I will be greeted with a smile and warm greeting when I arrive at work. This means so much to me. I want to thank you all for this, and let you know that I will remember this team as long as my memory holds out!

People sometimes don't get an opportunity to let others know how they have touched their lives....but I want to take this moment to thank you all for touching and adding such richness to mine.

When I am walking through a store in Montreal and not recognizing any faces or realizing that I won't have 'a gentle hand touch my arm' to give me a beautiful bright smile and warm friendly greeting...I will think of my co-workers / friends and will smile...even if no one knows why.

Thank you!
With my sincerest love
Tammy

I finally got to my condo, pulled into the drive port, shut off the car and gathered up my things.

Only One more day of this and then the man that had once again swept me off my feet with dreams of a happy life together and new adventures to share, will be here. We will be together. We rented a U-haul truck for all my things that were already packed to go. His parents, sister and her two kids will be staying at my condo and I will be staying at my sisters until after the wedding at which point Mack and I will 'honey moon' in a hotel. We have a couple things planned for everyone like a ride on the Century Queen around the lake, a wine tasting tour in Winfield, an old train ride in Westbank and dinner at a Japanese restaurant to name a couple things.

Once inside my condo after turning the lights on and placing my work paraphernalia in its prospective places, I went to the fridge to grab an ice tea.

I looked around my empty condo because everything was pretty much in boxes that filled the back bedroom, and sat at the table. All I had at the moment where my thoughts and a full can of iced tea.

I only seen my dad cry once in my life and really it was only watching a couple tears go down his face. But yesterday as we picked out his tux and met with the priest who was going to perform the wedding….he had tears fall then too. He was a man that worked so hard in life, made many mistakes yet survived to bring sound advice to me whenever I reached out to him. No one is perfect, but he is my hero in so many ways. I am going to miss him so much. He is happy that Jason and I are happy about having Mack become part of our family.

Mack, Jason and I were going to start our family together pretty much in a u-haul truck driving across Canada to an apartment above his parents place in Montreal.

My dad didn't like that too much. He told me that I should be careful to try to keep a little distance and privacy because he said living too close to in-laws sometimes is not good for a new marriage. He laughed and said you don't want your in-laws to become out-laws.

My phone announced a text came.

Flipping open the cell I read it.

"I love you and can't wait until I am with you again!" It was from Mack.

"I am so excited to become your wife Mack! I love and miss you too." I wrote back.

"We won't be apart again Tammy!"

"No, for the rest of our lives as long as God gives us, we can be together."

"I can't sleep."

"Neither can I."

"I love you."

"Ditto" I responded.

"I am going to hold you so close to me when I can and not let you go."

"I won't want to go Mack. I want to be in your arms every night, and be able to kiss you good morning every morning for as long as I can."

"I want to make you and Jason happy."

"You already have in so many ways Mack and I want to make you happy too."

"My wife, my love, I can't wait."

"Me neither, together again, together forever."

Mack phoned me and we talked for two hours on the phone before we were both almost falling asleep.

I dragged myself into the washroom at three in the morning to brush my teeth and get ready for bed. He will be flying into Kelowna in 36 hours, yet this time he will be leaving the Okanogan with a wife and son.

I will be leaving my family in the Okanogan valley for a new one in Montreal.

I sat on my bed and looked at the only thing left hanging in my closet. My wedding dress. My wonderful friend and sister in Christ, that Jason calls Aunty; had turned a dress that didn't quite fit me well, into one that was made for my body. I remember crying to my sister after I had picked it up and tried it on at home. It was beautiful but horrible on me. My matron of honor and wonderful life friend had worked a miracle with it. Yet for some reason I cried again after I put it on and saw how lovely it was on me when she was done with it. How blessed I was to have such supportive and loving people in my life. I lay down in my bed staring at the dress, knowing I would be wearing it soon, and that my life would never be the same again.

Thank you Father, I prayed. This was good. It was all going to be good, I thought as sleep finally took over and brought rest to my soul.

7

Montréal

We arrived. The rain that had been hitting the windshield harder and faster than the windshield wipers could aid in helping clear our visibility, stopped as suddenly as it had begun. The sun decided to make a bold statement in protest to the dark clouds trying to suffocate it, saying 'I am here'!

All three of us including my son's guinea pig, I am sure; sighed in relief as we made our last turn down the road that we would all be living on.

The streets were full of traffic and people seemed to be everywhere, on every street corner. They were crowding bus stops and at every cross walk waiting for lights to change. This was definitely going to be a place we were going to have to get used to. That is compared to the more laid back lifestyle of the sunny Okanogan.

We were all silent as the u-haul pulled to a stop in front of a side by side duplex right off a busy boulevard. It was two stories high when you don't count the basement belonging to the main floor dwelling. We would be living on the top floor.

Mack jumped out once the engine had been turned off and quickly ran over to greet his parents with a kiss. They must have been watching for us by the window because I was sure they were outside their door before we could get out of the truck.

We would be living on the top left side of the duplex. There were two doors standing side by side. One going into his parents' house and one that would lead up some stairs to our apartment.

Jason and I got out of the truck and stretched. I looked over to the doors on the other side of the duplex. I had gotten so tired of hearing about how the young girl next door was in love with him, that I finally told him that she would not be welcome in any place I live, if she was only interested in having a relationship with him. He on the other hand, sees no problem with her or her attentions towards him. "There was nothing he could do about it," he would tell me. What could I say to that? I suppose I was thinking about what I would do if a man had a crush on me. I would keep clear of him and discourage or even deny his entrance to my home. I thought if there was something that I could do about someone having a crush on me then there was surly something that he could do about it also. I greeted his parents as did Jason. Then the door to our apartment was unlocked for us to start placing the contents of the u-haul in our new home.

There was no real romance in unpacking.

Mack was happily chatting with his parents in French telling them about our trip across Canada. Then I heard the three of them making plans for dinner after we had dropped the u-haul off at the dealer. He told me we would be eating with his parents tonight in their place. I thought that that was nice of them to offer this to us, seeing as how we didn't really even have my dishes unpacked yet.

Then his neighbor came over all excited to see him back. Her and her mom came up and gave him a kiss and presented a welcome home gift to him. I stood there not knowing what to say. Should I be friendly and thus encouraging her to be part of my life? No. If she has such a big crush on Mack as he says she has, then I won't. I would know that she would not be coming over to get to know me. I thanked them for the gift but did not venture to make any indication I was going to invite them back. No promises of getting to know one another or any plans of future dinners or BBQs. I thought I was courteous like I would be to someone passing me on the street. Ready with a smile yet nothing more or less.

Jason was already in his room unpacking when they left. He had heard all about her too and wanted to prove he had no interest in getting to know the girl. Mack's parents went downstairs to prepare dinner so Mack and I were alone in the kitchen.

"I don't think they will want to come back after you were a bitch to them."

I stared at him in unbelief.

"Excuse me?!" I had never been called a bitch before. "I told you before we got here that I am not going to encourage a relationship with a neighbor that has a crush on you. I was not rude, but I definitely did not want to look like I would want to become friends either."

"They were happy to meet you, and glad to see me back." He looked as if he was trying to control himself.

"Mack, if you choose not to do anything about a young girls crush then you leave it up to me to deal with." I no longer felt like unpacking. "She is neither your family nor mine, or a friend of either of us. I feel no obligation to open my home to her."

"This is my parents' home and she grew up here!"

I could see that he was mad at me and felt at this point he would not defend or see my position, only hers. In his statement he so much as told me that 'this is not and never will be my home and she had more right to be in his house than I ever would'.

I stared at him, not understanding his anger and defense over her.

Maybe he is just tired from the trip across Canada just like Jason and me. Maybe that is why he is mad.

On the trip down when we stopped in Moose Jaw for dinner, I noticed that he protected the waitress too. I had ordered a meal and when it came she had gotten my order wrong. I wasn't mad about it. Yet, when I looked at Mack and told him that I would have to call her back and let her know about the mistake, his remark seemed a little defensive to me.

"Don't tell her she made a mistake it was the kitchens fault," He said. "I will eat yours and you can have some of mine if you want."

I got a little upset with that. What was the big deal? Just inform her she or him or they or them…..someone had made a mistake. Things like this happen sometimes in life, no big deal, but I wanted what I had first ordered. That is why a menu is handed to you…..to choose what 'you' wanted to eat. I was not mad at her, but why would I have to eat something I didn't want to eat? To protect her from knowing there was a mistake made? Why?

I gave in and ate a little off of his plate. He ate my meal. The waitress was never told of her mistake and received a large tip as thank you for her service. Aside from smiling at Mack several times I didn't see too much 'service' she gave that needed a large 'thank you' in money for.

Just like then for some strange reason I felt like somehow I was the bad guy here. Was I? Was I seeing everything all of a sudden in a wrong light? Maybe I was just tired and not thinking properly. Maybe I should not have worked until just before everyone came down and the wedding took place.

Even our supposed couple days in the hotel alone after the wedding didn't seem to work out as I thought it should. It was our only couple days alone after such a busy life changing time.

After the wedding and dinner party was over, we arrived late to the hotel. He knew the place had a pool so he informed me that while I changed for bed he wanted to go for a swim alone. No problem. Then the next day we had to

72

spend the rest of those days with his friends and family because they came all this way after all. Ok.....no problem. We would have the rest of our lives to spend time together right?

Yes, that was it. Maybe so much had happened so quickly that we were all just very tired.

Mack's dad came up the stairs to our place without knocking or announcing himself.

"Le souper est prêt….dinner is ready." He looked at me and smiled, apparently he was very proud of his use of the English language. I thought that was sweet of him to speak English for me and Jason.

"Jason, you ready to go have dinner with your grandparents?" I called out towards his open bedroom door.

He popped his head out from around the door with a smile and confirmed he was with a nod. "I am hungry." He announced, "What are we having?"

I looked at Mack's dad as he answered him. "We eat pizza."

Mack, Jason and I followed his dad down the stairs into their place where the table was set and pizza boxes were opened on the counter.

We ate while Mack talked with his mom and Jason and I were left to talk to his dad.

He was a very nice man but something about his repetition in saying the same thing over and over again reminded me of when I had worked in a locked dementia unit.

Yes. I am really, really tired, I thought to myself. I need to get the bed set up quickly and get a good night sleep.

After dinner, I was a little drained from what I felt, was having to keep Mack's dad occupied while he talked with and enjoyed his mothers company. Neither of them seemed to try to include Mack's dad in their conversation.

We said good night and went back upstairs. Jason went to get his bed ready in his room and Mack and I went to get the one ready in ours.

I brought some sheets into the room but stopped to look at a fully made bed set up in the room. Something bothered me about it.

One of the most important conversations I had with Mack when we discussed what I was going to bring with me from my place in Kelowna, and what I was going to sell....was the bedroom furniture. I told him that it was very important to me that I buy the bedroom suit to bring. We were starting a new life together and I wanted everything in the bedroom to hold only memories of the two of us. We both had past relationships but I felt this was going to be different. We were getting married and therefore committing ourselves to one another. To be honest, I also did not want to sleep on a 'stained' mattress. I had purchased a new bed, dresser and all the bedding for a new life with one man. I told him this request was not going to cost him anything because I was the one that was going to buy everything prior to the wedding and the move. I mentioned this several times because he told me that he already had a bed. He told me to sell Jason's and give Jason the new bed. I had already bought it. The whole bedroom was going to be new for a new marriage and life together. He argued back to me that he had bought a new bed and that I should sell Jason's because we didn't need another bed.

Something told me that this was not a new bed. Yet, why would he lie to me about it after I had already bought one? After I had told him that it was very important to me to start fresh.

I wanted to cry.

"This 'is' a new bed right Mack?" I asked him. "You promised me that this was a 'new to both of us bed right."

"I said YES to you, I don't have to say it a million times." He snapped back.

Why was he so rude when he spoke to me now? I wish he would have talked to me or treated me like this BEFORE the wedding! Because I don't know if there would have been one!

I looked at Mack. He was already in bed. His back was to me and it sounded like he was already sleeping. I sat down on the bed put the sheets on the floor that I had been holding and without even getting undressed, laid down praying for sleep to fill me with new strength for tomorrow.

"Tomorrow with be a new day," I told myself.

I closed my eyes and started to pray. I thanked Jesus for letting me marry the man that I loved. I asked Him to help Jason and I settle into this new life. I said the LORDS prayer, and then fell asleep.

The first couple weeks were full of dinners with different family members of his, yet when we were at 'home' dinners seemed to always be with his parents.

He drove Jason to the college and signed him up to start right away.

He drove me to the unemployment office where I successfully filed for UI.

I of course had to open a bank account for the checks to be deposited but found out that I needed Mack to sign for me to open one. That confused me because I thought, 'what if I was single and moved down here?' Would that mean that I would not be able to open a bank account in Québec on my own? I for some reason was not allowed to go onto his account, he said I had to open my own but have a joint one with him that was not linked to 'his' account.

Then we went to have our wedding pictures developed. He took me to this place relatively close to where we lived and even though the young woman greeted us in English, he started talking to her in french. I did not understand a lot of french so I felt a little left out. I stood there like a lump. They together decided on the pictures that would be developed and the different sizes available without my input.

He walked over to me when the woman walked away to do everything he requested of her.

"Why are you not talking to her in English and including me in some of this?" I was getting frustrated. "Mack they are my wedding pictures too!"

"Why would I ask her to speak in a language that isn't her own?" He said getting upset with me for even wanting him to do that. "It is easier for her to talk french."

"That is good that you are thinking of her." I was hurt now. "What about thinking of including me in this! She knows english, she greeted us with clear english when we walked in. What about how I would feel? These are my wedding pictures too!"

Now he was mad at me. "I am not going to ask her to speak English when I can speak french to her and just get this over with."

Now I was truly hurt. Again, I felt somehow like the bad guy. Maybe it was wrong of me to ask to be involved in this. Maybe it was wrong of me to think that my husband should be more concerned about how 'I' felt rather than a complete stranger! Shouldn't he think about what would be 'easier' for me rather than what would be 'easier' for a stranger.

She must have overheard some of the conversation because when she came back to give us the pictures and waited for us to pay…..she spoke in english. I smiled at her and said thank you. She smiled and said…."no problem."

We left the store. Mack got into the car ahead of me and slammed his door shut, turned on the ignition and without looking my way, waited for me to get into the car.

He drove the car fast and at some times drove a foot behind the car in front of us.

"What is the problem!" I asked him motioning at his angry posture and speed. "What is wrong with me wanting to be involved in some decisions? Or if someone can speak english, why can't we do business in english until I learn more french?"

"Shut the fuck up."

Silence.

I stared at him in disbelief. What did he just say! I did not deserve that? I had only been married around a month; maybe he thought I was starting to be a nagging wife? Was I nagging? I know I did not deserve to be sworn at. What do I do?

My head jerked to the side as he took a corner fast.

I don't know what to do. Who does he think he is that he can talk to me like that? I don't talk to him like that! And I definitely am not being unreasonable to ask my husband to show more concern for me than SOMEONE ELSE!

Once we got home. We again were invited down to eat with his parents. Once again the drinking started as soon as we walked in. Jason pulled me aside and asked if he had to eat with us and I told him no. He went upstairs to have a quiet supper alone. Once again, I was left to talk to his dad the whole dinner so Mack and his mom could visit with each other. Yet now I was certain that Mack's dad was suffering from dementia and was possibly bi-polar. I knew now that Mack could not handle the repetition or the emotional outbursts of crying his dad did every night. I now knew that I was there so he could enjoy a dinner with his mom and I would keep his dad out of his space.

The drinking continued, and I started getting sick. I felt like I was going to pass out. The glasses were constantly being filled and the last time I remembered drinking so much was almost 18 years ago. Since then I had maybe one bottle of wine a year. In fact half the time I went to finish the bottle it tasted like vinegar and I could then only use it for a meat marinade.

I made my way upstairs....to 'our place' to go to bed, my husband stayed with his parents drinking.

Maybe it was the difference in language but I was beginning to not know who I was anymore. I always thought I was a good cook and that people enjoyed my meals. Now I am told that the English do not know how to cook. It is for this reason of course that 'forces' Mack to cook when his mom is at work and hadn't been able to 'invite' us for dinner. I and my son are 'the bad guys again', because we had been told that because we like our meat medium, it is a waist to serve us good meat. THIS really hurt Jason. Even though I tried to let him know that it was perfectly fine to like meat done differently than someone else, he seemed to disappear inside himself. There were other comments made in reference to him not being good enough by just being himself. Somehow, he knew that these people would never accept him for who he was. This was the first change I seen in him that happened after our move to a "new life and new adventure!" We should have left then.

"You have changed too mom". Jason was staring out the window while lying on his bed one night. It was a night that his dad was getting drunk downstairs with his parents again, and very loudly yelling at them about how horrible 'we' were, especially Jason for some reason.

I sat on the edge of his bed. My heart was breaking for this young man, my son whom just wanted to have his dad in his life. Jason opened his arms up and decided to forgive his dad for not being in his life sooner, even though Mack never mentioned it or attempted to apologize for his absence. Jason opened his heart up to completely love and respect this man, a man now that appears to not be able to stand being in Jason's presence. So Jason; when his dad is at home stays in his room. This seems to piss Mack off. But then again…..it pisses him of when he is out of his room too.

"You were my mom that could stand up to anyone. Love everyone, and make all your own decisions." He rolled over a little to look at me. "Now, you apparently don't even know how to drive a car."

"If I still had my car (a car I bought new, on my own), I would pack what I could get in it right now and leave him."

"Not without taking me with you!" He exclaimed quietly.

"Of course not!" I responded and then drew him in for a hug while we both sat in silence listening to Mack yelling about what a no good useless idiot (of course all in french) that he thought his son was.

8

Rejection

I was sitting huddled into the door frame on the little open balcony overlooking the boulevard.

I watched the wind pick up speed, throwing little bits of garbage and tossing them in the air. The bits of garbage tried desperately to run away from this treatment to a different location along the sidewalks of the boulevard only to be found again by the merciless hands of the wind, picked up and tossed into the air again. This was not a battle the paper cups and torn newsprint could escape from. This was a battle that would be over when the wind decided it would be over.

Then the rain decided to join into the game.

Now the poor bits of garbage were getting it from all sides.

Dark rain clouds loomed arrogantly over the houses and buildings. There didn't seem to be an end to them. All summer long they hung like unwanted curtains in front of you. This was a repeat it felt like of last summer's weather. Finally releasing downpours of their content, making you feel desperate to know if the sun would ever come out again.

I pushed myself back into the door frame of the little second story balcony, trying not to get wet yet at the same time unwilling to get up off the door step to go inside from out of the rain.

What was I going to go into? I had finished cleaning the apartment, finished the laundry, finished phoning my dad to let him know what a wonderful time I am having in Montreal; and how happy I was to be here.

I wasn't going to go inside to just sit and watch TV. I hated just sitting and watching TV. I have never liked sitting in front of a television watching other people pretend to live life, when I knew that I was always happier living my life and doing things than just watching someone else live. At the notion of just sitting in front of the television, I always thought ......how long would someone just sit for, before they get bored and desired to get up off the couch to think of something they would like to do to enhance their life. How long would a person want to sit on a couch staring at a black TV? Would they willingly sit for a half hour? An hour? Three? Five? I personally think boredom would set in faster than they think. But.......now turn the TV on.....and you have people willing to waste so much of their life....time....just sitting and staring at a square box. I don't mean that this is never a good thing to watch an interesting program once in a while, but for me it was always just that....once in a while. I found so many other things I could be doing instead, so that I could live a more exciting life. I only used the TV for those moments in my life that ...well, where there were just empty pockets of time that needed to be filled. I also loved to learn and experience new things. So, if I knew that something of an educational purpose was going to be airing at a certain time then I would also make time to "just sit" and learn. Although, even saying that, I would still prefer to actually go to "see" a speaker than watch him/her on the TV.

I never used to think too much about the TV in either a good or bad way. It was not evil or good in my eyes; it just wasn't an issue to examine before. Now though, I find myself resenting the sound of it's ever presence in my life. My husband would come home from work after having met with clients, having lunch with them, working at an office he really didn't need to be at (he had a job where his office was "at home").Or from doing whatever it was he did because he rarely talked to me about what he did when he left the apartment. 'It was always boring and I didn't need to know'. Once again, my battle of trying to let him see it wasn't the "what" he was doing in his day I was interested in as much as I was interested in the "sharing" part of our lives together. I wanted to know and keep learning about "him". He never got it….I never needed to know…..I needed to stop asking questions…..I just needed to shut up. He did not have to talk to me about anything he did not want to talk about or that he deemed " boring"(although I felt that his word usage of "boring" meant….I don't want to tell you, don't ask). Then if he didn't have a shower as soon as he walked into the house then the next thing he did after walking into the apartment was turn the TV on. He didn't talk to me when he came home.

Then he would get up to cook supper on those few days we were not going down to eat with his parents. "The French knew how to cook", he would tell me in a manner that implied "the western people couldn't. He said as much at different times in different ways. In my stubborn response I would argue that I was a good cook and have been cooking all my adult life! I cooked for my son and anyone else that would come over for one of my meals. I was by no means a chef, but my food was good enough for other people to ask me for recipes to what I had cooked them. I loved having someone in the kitchen with me, talking with them and having that extra set of helping hands around to make things easier. I loved teaching my son how to cook and time the food so that everything is done at the same time. It was something that we could do to bond in. Talk about the day and or anything else that would come to our minds. Maybe we would discuss solving the world's problems or tell funny stories that didn't matter or just have words fall from our mouth with no other purpose other than to bond". I closed the door to offering to cook anymore. That part of me died. I "get it", I am a rotten cook.

The strangest things would come out of Mack's mouth though. He feels he needs to put me down and let me know how disappointed he is in me that "I don't cook for him". My brain cramps every time I try to tell him what he says to me about my cooking but he seems to have "chosen to forget that he put me down a million times over it". If there is one definite thing about Mack that I know for a fact is this…….HE NEVER FORGETS WHAT HE SAYS TO ME……HE CHOOSES TO SAY HE FORGETS IF IT SUITS HIS PURPOSE"! I have heard a million times him yelling at me and then the next day tell me that "he never said that", "that is not what he meant", or "ITS ALL IN YOUR HEAD"! So I started to repeat what he said to me right when he said it.

I had watched him play solitaire on his computer that never left his lap while he was at home, for almost two hours. Then I opened my mouth.

"Mack, why don't we do something together?" This was a mistake. He began yelling at me that I was the most boring person in the whole world and why would he want to do something with someone like me?

When he was yelling at me that I was the most boring person he ever met, I repeated it to him.

"You mean that I am the most boring person you ever met?" I would ask.

"YES! YOU ARE THE MOST BORING FUCKING PERSON I KNOW AND I WOULD RATHER DIE PLAYING FUCKING BORING SOLITARE THAN DO SOMETHING WITH YOU!!!!!!"

I repeated what I heard him say to me. "You mean that I am more boring than solitaire and you would rather die playing it than do something with me?"

"YES! YOU'RE BORING YOU FUCKING BITCH!"

84

At that point I could feel a knife slicing into my heart and chop out any ambitions to want to make this man be tormented from boredom by forcing him to want to do something with me. (This was a battle we fought for four years. I tried and failed. I tried and a piece of me died trying to get him to WANT to be with me.)He just didn't want to hear how much I wanted and needed him to share life with me.

Even when he cooks I need to stay out of the kitchen! My presence was only demanded when it came time to set the table and then Jason and I were made to sit down quietly for at least five minutes before the food was brought to the table. This was so strange to Jason and me. Everyone I knew from my grandparents down to aunts and uncles including my own parents never fought or got angry before sitting down to a meal. Kids where called when "supper was ready"; food was being put on the tables as we ran to wash our hands before coming to the table. We always ate around 5 o'clock. Dad would be cutting portions of meat at the table as we came to sit in our places. There was never any anger at the table.

With Mack though, he would have the right to be completely enraged with us if we were not sitting down....five minutes before the food came to the table. If we were not then we had ruined the meal. The food was a loss and so had his precious time been wasted on us. He would also (somehow in his brain) have the right, no; 'duty' to get mad at us and put our character down if we were not exactly where he wanted us when he wanted us to be there. If we did not compliment him on the meal at least two times, then he allowed us to know that we were not 'worth' his effort to make a good meal. We were ungrateful and unappreciative of the time he took to cook it. We were never allowed to just enjoy a meal and place more importance on the time in a meal that would bring a family together to talk and catch up with one another's lives. No, it was all about the food, his effort in cooking it for us, and listening to him talk….that is "IF" he wanted to talk to us. I no longer looked forward to sitting down to supper. Jason had closed up too. He had started to bring his mp3 player to listen to at the table because he could not stand the silence. Mack got pissed off with this also, yet couldn't he see "WHY" his son was doing it? Couldn't Mack "SEE" that he has made the "meal" more important than the people that were sitting down to eat it?

No…..

He would complain for hours to his parents telling them how ungrateful we were for everything he was doing for us. ….and they would agree with him.

This 'routine' was not immediate. We lost…I lost after many fights later trying to ask Mack if he would just try talk "with" us when we sat down to eat…not just talk TO us. This never worked, he didn't get it, and Jason starting shutting down, pulling away from him because the only thing he could hear his dad say about him or to him was what an awful son he was. Mack never wanted to get to know Jason, he just wanted to make Jason be and act in a way he decided he should be. Mack wanted Jason to like what he liked, think the way he thought and well…. be like Mack. I could not get Mack to see that he had an awesome son that held his own unique skills and wonderful personality. If it wasn't Mack's way, then it was stupid, worthless, waste of time and whatever the character trait, thought or action of disagreement was…..well …..without argument…..it just needed to stop! End of "discussion" (not that there ever was a true 'discussion' about anything he did not agree with). If Mack did not want to talk about something…YOU SHUT UP. You did not talk about it. Period! I was getting tired then, because if you do not solve little problems than those little problems become big ones, and you can't solve big problems by shutting the door and pretending they don't exist. A problem will not go away with ignorance. That undealt with mole hill will turn itself into a mountain. It's like the law of gravity, it will happen.

I went into the apartment once the rain slowed to a drizzle to get another cigarette and pour myself a glass of wine to bring out onto the balcony with me so I would not miss any ......what......so I would not miss any time spent out of the apartment.

I was smoking more than I had ever smoked in my life. I never really drank alcohol and used to get deathly ill after having two drinks on the rare occasion that I would have a drink or two. Now, my body seemed to be getting used to it.

"Another drink Tammy?" I stopped saying no, you were not heard anyway.

"Sure."

I closed the door behind me as I stepped out once again onto the little balcony, to once again settle myself down huddled up to the frame of the door to watch "other people" live.

Mack would come home when he wanted to. He would either have a shower or just go straight to his chair with his computer on his lap and not talk to me.

I took a long sip of my wine and then lit another smoke.

Jason had made a friend from a local church and was now at his friend's house.

I finished the glass of wine just as I seen Mack drive into the driveway. He looked up at me and said nothing. No wave. No hello. He reached into his car to grab his computer bag, closed the car door and turned to walk up the stairs that led into the front entrance down stairs. Before he got to the door though, the little neighbor girl came out of her parents place with a friend of hers.

"Bonjour Mack! Comme on ce va?"

He looked up and immediately showed a great big grin with a warm "hello" back and watched as the girls got into their small blue car before he continued into the house.

There was never any smile for me.

He must have decided just weeks after marrying me that I was not worth his kindness. Whatever he had imagined his life would be like with me and Jason before the wedding, it apparently was nothing like he dreamed. So, it …we…were no longer worth his effort of kindness or his time. We were now only there to be with him when he wanted us to be with him and not a second longer. We were only to speak when spoken to and not a word before or after.

One day he was watching a sailing show on TV that he had recorded. One that he could pause at any time he wished.

Sitting in his chair with his computer on his lap and the TV going, I tried to make a conversation with him.

Big mistake.

"SHUT THE FUCK UP! I AM TRYING TO WATCH THIS!"

I shut up. He yelled a couple more things pertaining to how ignorant I was and disrespectful.

I sat in the chair and told myself not to open my mouth.

After about 20 minutes he looked up and started telling me about some technique he just witnessed on the show that some of the men did with the sails and stated that they were stupid. He began telling me the right way they should be doing things.

He paused.

I looked at him and nodded my head in agreement. "Don't talk", I told myself.

Then his volcano erupted.

"I EXSPECT YOU TO TALK WHEN I TALK TO YOU!!!"

He yelled at me for almost 3 hours.

He yelled at me things like …"I was ruining the lives of children all over the world because I did not want to celebrate Christmas."

He got up from his chair to yell loader at me and pace in front of me pointing his finger in my face.

"YOU ARE A USLESS MOTHER AND HAVE RUINED JASONS LIFE!"

"I SHOULD HAVE RESCUE HIM FROM BEING RAISED BY SUCH A MESSED UP BITCH!"

"YOU THINK EASTER IS EVIL!"

"YOU KNOW NOTHING ABOUT SAILING!"

The list went on.

When he sucked his breath in for more yelling and put downs, I asked him very calmly to not yell. I told him that I was "right here and could hear him clearly enough without yelling". I said this to him very calmly almost five or six times. I knew that his parents could hear. But they didn't care. I knew the neighbors could hear. But they didn't care. I was just the stupid ungrateful English girl.

"Water off a ducks back" I tried to tell myself. Let these lies fall off of me. I am not the horrible person he is telling me I am. The words will fall off of me like "water off a ducks back". I tried to give myself a hug mentally. You are not this bad.

Finally my brain snapped.

"STOP IT! STOP YELLING! STOP IT!" I screamed so loud that almost no sound came out of my mouth. I grabbed my hair and wanted to rip it out so I could feel something other than this explosive ache in my heart. I started to cry….

Then….I saw him sit back in his chair, place his hands on the arm rests and then with a mocking arrogance he looked at me and said quietly and calmly…..

"Tammy………………………………..

…………..why are you yelling? I am right here" a smug satisfied grin showed itself to me as I looked unbelievingly at his face.

There was no question left in my mind. He hated me. He was not "out of control when he threw his temper tantrums. He knew what he was doing and what he was saying. He was completely in control and just wanted to hurt me any and every way and chance he could.

The door to downstairs opened. I got up from my spot on the balcony and went in to sit on the couch and wait for him.

He came up the stairs and entered the living area where I was sitting.

He went to sit in his chair and opened his computer on his lap.

"Do you want to sit with me?" I asked hoping I would not have to sit through silence.

He looked up. "Why? You never ask me questions like you do when Jason comes home because you don't care about my day."

There again was that contradictive speech of his. If I ask him questions, then he thinks I am a bitch; if I don't ask him questions….well, I am simply an uncaring bitch.

"How was your day?" I asked him.

He got up with his computer and came to sit beside me on the couch. The grip on his computer told me he couldn't think of any reason to say no to my request at the moment yet had no intentions of "sitting *WITH* me". He would sit next to me though. Does anyone else get the difference?????

"It was boring; I was at a meeting with a bunch of men."

I got closer to him. Then I smelt it.

"You smell like woman's perfume."

"What are you talking about?" he looked at me with anger.

I leaned closer to him. Then I saw it. Sparkling eye shadow was embedded into the curls of his very short hair that ran around his ears.

"Mack you have woman's make up in your hair and you smell like woman's perfume, then you tell me that you were only with men all day?" I moved away from him on the couch.

Here it comes.

"He threw his computer on the coffee table and began yelling at me. He yelled at me that I was nothing but a jealous bitch and a slut.

Then he told me that an old woman with glasses gave him a 'hug' today.

Unreal.

The only way you get makeup in your hair and smell like perfume is when you have skin to skin contact rubbing it on. Makeup will not travel through a pair of glasses and rub off into your hair if the only contact was a "quick kiss on the cheek".

I watched him walk into the bedroom then out again carrying some cloths and then slam the door to the washroom to have his shower. All the while calling me names and putting me down.

I walked into the kitchen to poor myself a glass of wine and grabbed my pack of cigarettes.

I once again found myself sitting huddled up outside against the bottom of the door frame on the little balcony overlooking the boulevard. I looked up into the clouds to see if they knew what they wanted to do. Drizzle or rain? I looked down at the wet pavement and noted the wind was calmer. I saw the wet, dirty bits of garbage clinging to the spots they had been flung too by the wind and drowned by the rain.

I knew he would not say another word to me for the rest of the evening, or when we went to bed.

9

Elementary School

"Nice of you to decide to take five more minutes for your lunch break ladies. Now you will have the whole class wait for five minutes past dismissal." This was said in french, there was to be NO english spoken in this class at all! This was made to be quite clear right from the start.

My two newly found friends and I grimly moved to our seats with our tails between our legs. Planting our buts firmly in chairs at a table that we had claimed as our own, without smiling we stared straight ahead at the chalk board in the front of the class.

I did not know what my two friends were thinking, but I was livid. The Chinese restaurant across the road from the school became busy just as we wanted to leave, so we were unable to get our bill to make it back on time. Five minutes! Resentment started to build in my heart.

I was treated like a nothing by my husband and his family and now that I found out the Quebec government stated I would be unable to work in this province without passing an in-depth French test; I felt the province was treating me like a nothing also.

My husband was enjoying the fact that he did not have to be with me Monday through to Friday from 8 a.m. to 4 p.m. I surmised this because when I was at home, he was not. "He had to work!" he stated angrily. Now that I was 'sent' to French school I noted that he all of a sudden was at home pretty much all week working out of his home office. I know this because every time my friends or I would drive somewhere for lunch we drove by my house. It was a going bet at the beginning to see if he was home, because I was not. This was in no way a coincidence! Working consisted of watching movies, doing errands that he wanted and well just doing what he wanted to do. I also found out that his ex came by to 'visit' the little mouse of a dog they had together while I was in school. This I found out through a slip of the lips from his mother. Or was it a slip of the lips. I was crying from one of his verbal attacks on me one day and had told his mom and dad that if I had the money I would leave their son. She responded readily that she would give me the money I needed to leave him. Unfortunately the vow I made before God came screaming back into my head.....for better or worst..... I didn't realize that worst would come so quickly in this marriage and last for so long.

I looked over at one of my friends; she was almost close to tears trying to understand what she was being told while looking at her French workbooks. We were not even allowed to offer an explanation of something in English to one another; it all had to be in French. She was an LPN that had worked in the hospital in Calgary for years. She was older than I was and was just as frustrated as I was to find that we were not allowed to work here without passing 'the test'. I glanced over my shoulder to see my other friend writing in her workbook. She seemed to be able to grasp French faster and was determined to pass 'the test'. She was a doctor that had specialized in skin disorders and again was older than I was by about three years. Now, we were treated like uneducated simple minded children.

I felt trapped, unwanted, unloved, misunderstood and constantly in a position of defending and protecting my son from the onslaught of verbal and recently physical abuse.

"We are going on a field trip this Friday to a grocery store so the class will learn how to shop for food". (said in french).

My mouth dropped open. My dignity was crushed yet again. My pride pricked.

"Learn how to shop!?!?!" My friends and I looked at each other in amazement. We all had raised children and ran a household for years which I believe included shopping for food. Now, it appears that we are in need of learning how to shop. I suppose it was no different than last month we were in need of an outing to go and learn how to visit and use the library.

"Now class, we are going out to practice our directions" (in French).

Everyone was called out of their seats to line up by the door. We obeyed. Then we were to walk quietly down the hall in single file to the staircase and then finally outside. Once outside we again were asked to stay together while she gave us some more instruction in French.

"You will get a partner and take turns verbally directing the other person to the bakery and back here keeping along the sidewalk. When you get back to the front door of the school you will then direct your partner around the school back to the doors again. After this you will change position and the person that was being directed becomes the director. You will go to the bakery and then around the school again. When you are done you will wait at the front doors until the whole class has finished.

My LPN friend and I joined up.

I looked at her and smiled saying in a hushed English voice, "fun fun!"

I think because my grasp of French was a little larger than hers I took the lead.

Mon ami, tu dois turner a droite. Puis, tu continue tout droit. Arête. Maintenant tourne à gauche. Continue tout droit. Arête. S'il te plait, continue tout droit avec moi." I was also motioning with my hands in the direction she needed to go and when I told her to stop I opened my hand to stop.

By the time we had gotten to the back side of the school we took that opportunity to talk and just walk with each other. We noted that a lot of the other 'students' were also taking that opportunity to talk to one another in their own languages.

"I don't get this," she exclaimed in frustration. "I don't think I am going to understand this enough to ever pass a government French test." She looked very depressed at that moment.

"You will! Look at what you have done up to now in your life! This may be hard girl but you have gone through harder things in life." I smiled at her and gave her a quick hug. "Think of those situations that you have had to work through. The co-workers that made you miserable or a moment in your children's lives that forced you to meet with teachers or doctors. You did it. Those times are over and when you really examine those moments then 'you' will notice that you did it. You lived through them and some of them even made you a stronger person whom is now able to take on different challenges'."

I didn't know if I was trying to encourage her or myself, but I knew we really had no choices right at this point in our lives other than to live through this humiliating experience.

"They make you feel like they are doing you a favor by giving you $200 a week to come learn French." She stopped and looked me straight in the eyes, "I would have gotten more money on UI alone than what they give me now. I have not been this broke in years!"

"I know how you feel," I told her with a little self pity tinged in my voice. "I get an allowance of $20 dollars per week from my husband. That is the same amount that Jason gets. Mack is acting like we should be grateful to get anything because neither one of us are working right now, but if you really look at the situation, than this is not our fault!" Now I started getting mad. "Jason has put his resume in at least a million places and has been refused and even put down for trying to get work because he does not speak French. We were told getting a job here was going to be no problem!" I waved my hand in the air, "This is not our fault that neither of us is working right now! We have both been sent to school and to make things worse for Jason, the college has refused to take into account anything he did in BC and told him that he would have to start back in grade 10 courses!"

Boy did I ever flip fast. I went from trying to encourage her out of her depression and anger over her situation to joining her in her woe is me moment.

"I gave up a good job and my home for a bunch of broken promises." She sighed heavily and her shoulders sank with an unseen weight that I knew would not be lifted soon.

"I know how you feel." We both stood still lost in our own thoughts of sorting out how we actually got ourselves into this life position.

I noticed that there were just a few of us left behind the school so I thought we had better get going again.

"Come on lets hurry back to the front of the school so we can get this over with."

"Yes." She agreed and we both hurried around the side to the front of the school where once again I started telling her in french how to walk to the doors.

Half of the class was already starting on the next round switching partners.

My friend looked at me and started with her commands.

"Commence," she commanded like a drill sergeant, and I like her disciplined soldier stepped high in the direction she told me to go towards the bakery.

We started to laugh at the way passerby's on the sidewalks and in cars driving the boulevard next to the school were looking at us.

"The kindergarten class is out of the building," I whispered in English.

Once we were in the back of the school again we took another 'break'.

When the class had finished their walk and everyone was gathered up and made to stand in a quiet line up. We all filed back into the school, up the stairs, down the hall, into our classroom without a sound and back into our seats.

The lesson continued.

I looked up to see the clock above the chalk board which told me that I had another twenty minutes of class left (five of those being the 'detention' minutes). Awesome, but then; I go home.

I wonder how Jason's' day was going. I wonder if Mack is also looking at the clock and mourning the fact that he had to come pick me up soon.

I found myself slipping more and more into silent thought.

I went from one prison to the next with no break. To no one that cared. School then home. To do nothing. There was no 'school bell' that rang, just the teacher telling us we were dismissed.

I gathered my books up and walked out of the class along with everyone else.

The school was mainly young people that were kicked out of their schools for various reasons and had to come here to finish their education.

I walked out of the school and looked around for Mack.

There he was ....sitting in his car watching three young women in front of him smoking, talking and laughing.

I paused. Would he look around to see if I was coming? I was already technically five minutes late. Would he look around to search for me? I stood there on the sidewalk of the school steps and waited.

No.

I waited.

His eyes never left the young girls.

"Tammy," I told myself; "why are you waiting?" I knew that I was not as interesting to him as the girls before his eyes were. Sadness filled my heart. Then anger started to replace it.

I marched up to the car and got in. He never even looked at me. He started the car and backed out of the stall he was parked in.

Silence.

No, 'how was your day'. No interest in me at all. I looked at his stone like unfriendly expression that was now on his face. Not the same one he had when he was watching the young women. I don't think he is going to tell me about his day or ask me about mine.

"Did you want me to introduce you to the girls?" I asked blandly after putting my seatbelt on and positioning my bag with all my books in it by my feet.

"What the fuck are you talking about?" "What girls?" "I didn't SEE any girls!"He pushed on the gas to shove himself into the flow of traffic budding in front of an oncoming car to enter the boulevard.

"I didn't SEE any girls you fucking paranoid jealous bitch!" He switched gears making the car violently change gears which made me jerk around in my seat. He sped up and started weaving dangerously in and out of traffic. "You are fucking insane!! I married you! I am not interested in anyone else! I don't SEE other sluts!"

'No, no never!' I rolled my eyes and stared out the side window. Go ahead Mack. Drive crazy. If you kill us ……..it will all be over. I wasn't living now and neither was my son. I hated Mack when he would 'play with words'. He was staring right at those girls. Does he enjoy lying? So maybe he means…..'I looked' or 'I saw' the girls but because he wants to be mad he tells me he never 'seen' the girls. Talk about an insecure manipulator.

Why are you with me Mack? Don't tell me this is love. I stared straight ahead asking him questions in my head that I knew he would not answer if I asked them out load.

He sped up to run an orange light that had changed to red as we got there.

I sat staring ahead.

Finally home. He slammed on the breaks in the driveway, jumped out of the car, fiercely slammed the car door, walked up the stairs to his parent's entrance and went into their home slamming the door behind him.

I unbuckled my seat belt, opened the car door, reached slowly for my bag and got out of the car. Closing the car door with only the amount of normal force needed to do so, I started up the stairs to the entrance door leading to our place on top of his parents.

Once inside, the silence hit me. "Welcome home!" It said as if the very air in this place had become my friend. My heart was breaking and tears slowly trailed down my cheeks.

After allowing myself a small couple minutes to cry, I wiped the tears away and told myself that was enough tears for the day.

I put my bag away and walked into the open kitchen. He had eaten out today. The kitchen was still clean. "Nothing for me to clean here," I said to myself. Turning I walked into the living room part of the open space. I saw a couple rental movies on the coffee table. One apparently was still in the player. "I better not move them," I thought to myself and continued my search for something to clean or do.

I sat on the coach.

I heard Mack yelling at his parents downstairs about what a "crazy, fucked up, insane person I was".

Was I?

Had everyone in my life just pretended to like me? Did everyone think of me this way? Mack's family appeared to just be devastated for him that he married me and had to cope with a horrible son and wife.

He kept telling me that he had no other problem in his life but me and my jealousy.

Really!

Then why does he have a problem with his son? Jason has no jealousy issues with him.

Why is his dad 'afraid' of him?

Why do his friends jump when he speaks and then say…."that's just Mack".

Why has his family made several comments on "when Mack wants something he wants it now without thinking of anyone else."

Why do I hear comments on how much you and your ex fought and yelled at each other all the time?

Why does your mom have so many stories about how much you got into physical fights all through your school years?

"OF course no one opposes you within the circle of your family and friends Mack, they hate seeing your temper."

"It is not my "jealousy" that you don't like Mack," I thought realistically. "You don't like that 'I' am asking you to be a husband that is interested in his wife!"

He has lived all his life being admired and told how good looking he is, and getting what he wants; that he doesn't know how to handle.............'responsibility'.

He has never been 'responsible' to another person, a child or a committed relationship. He has never had to think about someone else. He honestly has not had to 'protect' or 'defend' or 'support' someone other than himself.

His ex girlfriends (one was a model); all had that same self centered way of thinking. Vanity, vanity and more vanity. I can almost guarantee that not one person in his world ever thought about subjects like 'feeding the hungry' or 'sheltering the homeless'.

The screaming and yelling died down a bit as I heard a movie start up down stairs.

I looked around again.

Yip, he has had a hard day. It looks like he went out for lunch along with whatever else or whoever else he was with, then after going to a video store to rent some movies came home to watch them. Now, he will come up after he has eaten with his mommy and watched a movie so he can "relax away from horrible me" at which time he will be drunk and crawl into bed.

Then he will sleep. Not touch me, because "I repulse him", and sleep a dream filled sleep that too will not include me.

Yip, he loves me.

I got up off the couch, grabbed my school bag and went to the kitchen table to start doing my 'homework'.

Three sentences later and that task was done.

After putting everything away, I looked at my options.

I can't go anywhere; I have no car, money or 'permission'.

I went back into the kitchen, poured myself a glass of wine, went out onto the tiny front balcony overlooking the boulevard, lit a cigarette and watched the cars go by.

10

Quitting

The snow was piling up on my little balcony. Quickly pushing the small shovel around to force the snow through the railing took only a couple minutes. It fell heavily to the front entrance below.

Leaning the shovel against the wall beside the door, I went back into the apartment, grabbed my school bag and headed for the front door.

The snow kept falling in huge fluffy flakes that reminded me of cotton balls. I raced across the road through salt filled slush that somehow made its way through the sewing in my boots. The bus stop was almost right across the road from our place, yet it felt too far away for my liking this morning. I was already cold and miserable standing next to the bus stop and I had only been there for five minutes before the bus pulled up to let me on.

Once in the bus, I pushed the ticket through the appropriate slot and grabbed onto the pole to stand next to the door. The bus was full as usual and I found myself pushed up against a couple people also clinging to the same pole.

Wonderful.

The ride took around 30 minutes to reach the school. As often as it stopped to let people off, more people came on to fill their spots.

I squeezed out of the bus and back into the morning snow storm. There were very few people outside the school this morning, only a couple hard core smokers. I didn't think I needed to have one bad enough to stand outside in this misery so I speedily headed for the front entrance.

Just as I was about to step onto the front steps I heard a car horn and like everyone else turned to see who it was.

A small East Indian man waved at me from behind the steering wheel of an Oldsmobile.

I smiled at him and turning, raced now in his direction. He leaned across the seat and reached for the passenger door to open it for me, indicating with another wave that he wanted me to get into the car with him.

I jumped in and closed the door shutting out the heavily falling snow.

"I am glad to see that you made it today!" Rubbing my hands together to warm them up I reached for a cigarette that he was offering me.

"Yes, it is bad weather today. Very bad. I am going to leave after the first break in class to make sure I will make it home. They should not have school today!" My friend stated.

"Well maybe it will be like the last snow storm and they may close the school again early before it gets too bad outside for people to drive." I wishfully countered.

My friend had almost quit coming to school because he found the hours to be too long. He correctly observed that after lunch everyone just sat around and 'practiced' their French with one another. This was a waste of time and like he said…. "We have families and some of us have jobs too, why do they make us sit here just to fill time?"

We talked casually as we smoked our cigarette.

Everyone agreed with this statement, except the instructors. When the students started to complain about this their defense was telling us that 'we get paid to be here so we should not complain and be thankful to the Quebec government for the privilege of being here.'

"I brought you some curry rice my wife made last night, it is very good. You eat it for your lunch Tammy, you will like it." He was very pleased with himself that he could offer me this kindness, and I was warmed by him and his wife's thoughtfulness.

"Thank you, you are too kind to me!" I took the Tupperware container full of an orange color blend of rice and vegetables and placed it in my bag.

"No, you are a good friend Tammy." He gathered his books up after shutting the ignition off that had been running and keeping us warm, and then reaching for the door handle he looked at me and said, "You ready to run to the door?"

"As ready as you are!" We both ran to the front entrance of the school slipping at least a dozen times along the way, but made it through the doors into the school without falling.

Again not too many students were in the school. The large room that we were all supposed to have our breaks and eat our lunch in was almost empty of people.

"Maybe they are all upstairs in their rooms?" I offered an explanation to an unspoken question as I noted my friend looking around the almost empty room.

"Yes, you want to go up too?" he asked.

"Not really but we may as well." I answered.

Both of us turned and went up the stairs. As we were walking down the hall towards our class we again noticed that there were few students up here also. We went into our classroom, greeted the instructor in French and sat down at our table. There were only three other classmates in the room.

"No one else wanted to brave the snow to get here today hm." I whispered in english to my friend which immediately got a frown in my direction from the instructor.

I smiled and slouched in my seat as a response.

Without saying a word to us, she got up and left the room.

I unpacked my books and placed them on the table along with a pencil, eraser and pen. All five of us sat in silence and waited for her return.

After 15 minutes she came back into the room and announced in French that the school was going to be closed today due to the snowstorm and dismissed us to go back home.

I packed my bag back up and after talking to my friend for a couple minutes downstairs I once again was standing in the heavily falling snow by another bus stop.

The bus ride home was as crowded as the one coming. This time it took me 45 minutes to get home because this bus stopped a block away from my home. By the time I got into the house my boots were soaking wet and my feet were frozen.

Putting my bag down in its place, I sat down on the couch, listened to the silence and stared at the floor.

'I am not going back there,' I thought to myself. I had been going for about a year and felt depression slowly settle itself into my life. My LPN friend had already quit and hired a private tutor to help her with her French. She finally got a job doing what she was trained to do with the understanding that she would continue her French lessons and try to take 'the test' after one year of her employment.

The next 'field trip' my class was scheduling was to another humiliating degradation of our intelligence I believed.

I got up from the couch and went to my school bag remembering the curry rice my friend had given to me. I walked into the kitchen and put the container in the microwave then opened a drawer to get a fork. The microwave announced a minute and a half had passed and shut itself off. I took the container of rice out and went to the table. After sitting down at the table slowly eating the delicious gift, I thought about my husband that was in Toronto for a meeting with a client right now. I thought about my son that had been kicked out of the house and was now staying with a friend. I thought about why he had been kicked out.

For no good reason. The lists of Jason's offenses according to Mack were numerous. He didn't come to the table fast enough for dinners. He had his mp3 player in his ears all the time. He kept leaving hair in the sink after he used the washroom in the morning. He stayed in his room too much. When he was out of his room he played his hand held game too much. He didn't want to help his grandparents take care of the yard by mowing the grass or shoveling snow. He didn't want to go downstairs when we had our many meals down there with them. After making himself something to eat in the kitchen he didn't clean up after himself soon enough. He would on the occasion forget to close a cupboard door in the kitchen after taking something out of one. He would ask for rides from Mack from time to time when he ran out of bus tickets. He would ask for Mack to buy him bus tickets. He didn't say thank you for dinner as often as he should. He didn't compliment Mack's cooking as often as Mack thought he should therefore according to Mack he did not appreciate the food or the time it took Mack to cook it. It was as if we would 'smack Mack in the face' and tell him we didn't appreciate what he just did for us, (according to Mack that is). He would drink too much coke which somehow really annoyed Mack.

After one of his drinking rant fests downstairs with his parents over what a horrible son he had, I got called downstairs for 'the lecture' the next day.

"Jason is the boss of the because!" Mack's dad would say to me. He would then go on and on about how horrible Jason is.

Finally I got really mad at them one day. Why was I putting up with this shit! Who are they to talk to me about my son!

"What do you want me to do?!" I yelled at them one day in anger. "Start putting him down like the rest of you people and leave him absolutely no one in his life right now that cares for him!? Why don't I go get him and bring him down here right now so we can all just start calling him names and slapping him around!"

I started pacing in front of them and my anger built more when Mack's mom had the balls to say to me…. "No we don't mean that Tammy we all love him."

WHAT! This was by far the strangest way I ever knew of to show someone you love them!

"My son left his family and friends to come here!" I raised my voice and continued, "He was excited to come here! He opened his heart up to all of you and forgave and loved his dad without even thinking about it or being asked to forgive!" I moved towards the door to leave.

Just before I opened the door to get away from them I threw one more angry statement out to them. "I WILL NEVER STOP SUPORTING AND DEFENDING MY SON! I WILL NOT JOIN YOUR 'LETS ALL BASH JASON' PARTY!!!" I went out of their house, ran up the stairs to our apartment and straight into my son's room.

My son was crying into his pillow. My anger towards them was now sealed in my heart. I sat on the bed next to him and gently pulled him into my arms.

"I am so sorry that I married him! I am so sorry that I brought you down here! You are an awesome person Jason! Don't let these people hurt who you are! I love you so much!"

"They all hate me!" he cried into my shoulder. "What did I do to make dad hate me so much!"

"They hate you because of your dads' jealousy over you. He may have imagined that you would be going out to nightclubs and bringing young people over to his place. He thought you would be more dependent on him and his vast supply of wisdom, not a fully dependant young man with your own dreams and ideas that.....dare I say.....are different than his! Your dad hates the relationship that you and I have, he hates that you don't like or do everything that he likes, he is jealous of you and he hates that!"

"I hate it here!" he stopped crying and looked at me. "I hate it here!"

I remember the last straw for him was when he had asked to drive the car to a job that he finally got, cleaning the pools at a water slide park at night. It was in the evening and Jason was going to need more practice hours driving the car because he was going for his test soon. So, Mack and I borrowed his dad's car and let Jason drive to work.

After about 30 minutes into the drive to his job which normally took an hour, there were two other cars that we were driving along side that were coming off of the merge lane. Jason let the first one go ahead of him and the other car slowed down to go behind Jason joining the highway. Mack freaked out.

"You fucking stupid!" Mack yelled at Jason. "Pull this car over right now!" Mack punched the interior dash and swore again at Jason.

Jason's whole body stiffened and he grabbed the steering wheel tighter in his fists.

Mack went to grab the wheel and tried to pull it in the direction of the side of the road. We were on a highway that the speed limit was 120 and there were cars all around us.

Jason gripped the steering wheel even harder and tried to keep the car on the road. "We can't just pull over here!" he emphatically replied.

Mack again continued with his barrage of verbal name calling, punching the interior of the car and then reached for the emergency break pulling it up as hard as he could.

"What do you think you are doing!" I demanded from the back seat. Mack was the dangerous out of control person in this car right now, not Jason. He was the one with his inappropriate rage that was possibly going to get us killed.

Thankfully the emergency brakes were completely worn out! That could have put us into a deadly spin at high speed on a busy highway if they had worked!

"Just let him get to a safe place to pull over!" I yelled at the still snorting Mack.

His blood vessels were bulging in his neck, his face was red and he kept punching and hitting things. Then he reached for the ignition keys.

Jason finally threw the car at a screeching halt to the side of the road. "Are you crazy!" he said to his dad and jumped out of the car.

I jumped out too. "What did he do that was so wrong?!" I yelled at Mack.

"He is not driving safely! That car coming off of the merge had to slam on his breaks behind us!" Mack yelled back along with a string of swearing and name calling.

"The other car did not have to slam on his breaks and I would have done no different to let the cars merge onto the highway than Jason did!" I replied. "YOU are the one that almost got us killed and who knows who else!"

Mack jumped into the car and demanded that I get in also. He said Jason can go fuck off.

"I am not getting into a car with you right now!" I was getting extremely frustrated and completely upset with Mack thinking that he could drive like a lunatic in his anger while someone else was in the car, especially when that 'someone else' was me. (Which was almost every time I was with him in the car now; Mack used the car to prove how mad he was at me all the time.) Now though, the biggest reason for me not to 'get into the car' with him was that I was not going to just dump my son off on this highway and leave him here for NO GOOD REASON! A grown man having an unreal temper tantrum was no good reason. Even if I had a good reason I would not just kick someone out of a car alongside the highway! Especially my son!

Mack at one point tried to physically put me in the car and slammed the car door on me before going around to the drivers' side. I jumped out again.

Jason had yelled at him; "let go of my mother!" Jason again yelled at Mack to leave me alone and get his hands off of me.

To which Mack started yelling back with hateful sarcasm…."Oh, you want me to let go of your mommy!"

There were more verbal exchanges between Mack and I before Jason and I started walking together.

Mack followed close behind in the car.

We had walked for about 15 minutes in silence when Jason in frustration quietly said "I wish he would stop following us! Screw off dad," and without turning he gave Mack 'the finger'.

That was all Mack needed. I did not see Jason 'give the finger' and was startled by Mack all of a sudden accelerating and racing up in front of us, slamming on his breaks, jumping out of the car and coming directly after Jason to physically assault him.

After unsuccessfully trying to get Mack off of his son, I grabbed my cell phone and called 911. I think now that one of the cars passing us may have called ahead of me because the police were there fairly fast.

When Mack knew the police were on their way, he released Jason and walking over to the car and leaned casually against the trunk.

I ran to Jason's side where he was now sitting on the gravel with a torn shirt and splatters of blood.

A cop pulled up, took a couple seconds to do something in his car then got out and walked over to Mack. He carefully looked at Jason and I sitting in the gravel as he passed us.

Mack was already talking in a calm manner to the cop in French telling him that his son had been driving dangerously. Mack said he asked Jason calmly to pull the car over and let him drive the rest of the way to work. He told the cop that Jason refused and became rude and ignorant to him.

I could not believe what I was hearing!

"That is not true!" I proclaimed in french to the officer.

This went back and forth but the cop believed the calm and gentle speaking 'dad'. Not me. Mack was also telling him that we were from BC and hated French, and that I would lie and stick up for my son. That he was the poor frustrated dad just not knowing how to deal with this sad situation. He also told him that we just had gotten married and he and his son did not have a good father son relationship. That is why his son is so rebellious towards him and I am lying for my son.

That may not have been the perfect translation of his exact words, but it was definitely what he was implying and saying in French to the officer.

Jason didn't say a word, just sat there in the gravel holding his head.

We lost to everyone out here! It is apparently quite okay with everyone to be so crazy mean to us ignorant English people.

The cop asked if we had anyone to pick Jason up, he didn't want the two of them together until everyone calmed down. I had no one so Mack gave me his cousin's phone number.

I phoned Mack's cousin to pick Jason up then the police took Jason to a safe spot to wait. In front of the officer I made Mack promise that he would not drive dangerously, to which he stated "I never drive crazy or angry Tammy, you know that".

Unbelievable! He could lie with a straight face, a calm manner and …..smile!!!!!!!

And to this day he will not admit the truth of how that event took place. Mack wants to believe he does no wrong, so to him; it was Jason that became enraged and started driving recklessly and he (Mack) was just trying (of course out of worry for his son) to control his out of control son.

I finished the rice and got up to take the bowl to the sink to clean it up and put the container back in my school bag.

When that was completed I again went to the couch to sit down.

I never imagined that my son would leave my house like this. I thought it would be an exciting adventure after he finished school, got a job and found a place to live on his own. I imagined that I would help him move and decorate his own place. Not, send him out without finishing his schooling, not enough money to support himself and no place to live.

I remembered another time when it was dark out and miserable with heavy rain when I got a text from Jason saying there had been a bomb threat in the subway and everyone was kicked off down town Montréal. He didn't know where he was, couldn't speak French and didn't understand too much of the instruction on where to go or how to get there.

I panicked and told him that I would come to get him. I asked him what he was close to. He told me that his phone was out of money and he was near the Eaton Centre. I hoped my text would get to him and sent off a message telling him I would be there in an hour. That was how long it would take me if I left right now.

I told Mack what had happened and that we needed to go now!

Mack was warming up some milk to try make cheese and told me straight out that he was not going to throw the milk out and just 'run' because Jason wanted us to.

"He doesn't ask for rides a lot and this is not a typical situation!" I almost yelled at him. "We have to go get him! He is out of minutes on his phone doesn't have any money and can't understand anyone around him. It is dark and raining out! I want to go now!"

"I am not throwing this milk out." He stated again.

"Get your mom up here to watch it while we go get him!" I replied astonished that 10 dollars worth of milk was more important to Mack than his own son.

Mack was not going to go. Period.

I raced downstairs and let myself into his parents' house quickly begging them to use their car. I told them why I needed it and they ran to the TV and turned the news on, then amazingly enough sat down to watch the live coverage of what was happening downtown.

They wanted to watch the news first and said that they were sure Jason could make it home on his own.

'Am I trapped in twilight zone,' I started getting sick.

"I told him that I would go and get him! I can't text him back because he doesn't have any more minutes on his phone and has no money. How is he going to get home!

I argued and begged Mack and then his parents for two hours. No one wanted to go get him.

I could not help my son! I had no money or car. He was waiting in the dark, windy, rainy night and I could not get to him or even let him know what was happening. I should have been there a long time ago. I never gave up; I ran to Mack's parents and then back to Mack. They told me he could take a cab. I told them that he did not have any money!

Finally Mack's mom gave in and got into the car with me to go almost 6 hours after I told Jason I would be there.

It was almost midnight and seven hours after he asked me to come get him when I finally showed up at the Eaton Centre where we were supposed to meet at.

Jason was no were to be seen.

We drove around and I continued to pray and ask God to protect him. I was almost in shock with worry and grief. I was also seething at Mack and his parents for being so cold towards my son.

Finally almost one o'clock in the morning driving back home without Jason, I got a call on my cell from home.

It was Jason. He was sick, wet and frozen but he was at home! He was understandably upset and asked me where I was and how come I did not come to pick him up after I had told him that I was going to?

What could I say! I tried Jason! I really tried hard to be there!

I was so happy to hear his voice and couldn't get home fast enough to let him know that I loved him and that I was so happy he was ok.

'I tried Jason', I said to the empty living room. My heart began to ache as I remembered how I just couldn't seem to be there for my son anymore. Sadness and depression threatened to take over my moment of reflection.

I got up from the couch and went into the kitchen to make myself a cup of instant coffee, grab a cigarette then again go outside onto my little balcony. The snow had already piled up so much again on it that it looked as if it hadn't been shoveled off this morning.

I now didn't care about the snow or the cold. Pushing myself up against the door frame as much as I could, I again thought of Jason. Where was he in this storm?

I guess I didn't try as hard as I could have. I failed you somehow, and don't know what to do now.

After my cigarette, I came in and looked at my bag. It was still leaning against the wall by the stairs leading to the main entrance of the apartment.

Jason quit school. He said that it was made quite clear to him that no matter what courses he was to take and how long he stayed in school he was not going to get any certificate unless he too passed a French test.

I didn't blame him. Then, I thought that maybe I could learn something from his stand on rejecting 'the test'.

I went over to the coffee table where the phone was and picking it up quickly dialed the schools number. After 4 rings it went to answering machine, so I left a brief but to the point message. "This is Tammy; I would like to inform the school that I will no longer be attending…….. I quit."

11

Poetry and Painting

My mind seemed to be the only thing that was busy these days. I needed my hands to be busy also. There was only so much cleaning I could do in this little apartment. Sometimes I thought that you could literally eat off of my floors. Everything was dusted, watered, washed, dried, organized and sometimes rearranged almost daily. The only thing I did not have to plan is meals. Even the area around the base of the toilet got a daily wipe down. The garbage bins had no time to fill up before I was emptying them. Then I sat.

Once in a while I would sit at the computer and send my resume out to cyber world job postings. I even got a job offer taking care of someone's dad. It would have been in their home. I didn't like the low wage offer or some details of the job description though. I think because I am familiar with all the rules and regulation and possible hazards of going into someone else's home to do personal/medical care, I didn't like the wishy washy outline of duties. I didn't take it. If and when I leave this province I did not want anything to stain my reputation and possibly make it hard later on in life to get a job elsewhere.

I needed something more to fill my mind and my hands. So I started to write little stories.

THE SPARROW QUESTIONS THE FOX

'I want to feel cherished,' said the sparrow to the fox

The fox looked up and said 'you need to be different.' You know, set apart from the rest.'

The sparrow and fox watched as an eagle flew high over their heads.

'Can you fly as high as the eagle' he said?

'Well, no.' the sparrow admitted sadly.

'Then I want to feel beautiful,' the sparrow proudly said as she tilted her brown little head.

The fox smiled and said….'you mean like a parrot or bird in paradise?'

The sparrow looked down at her plain brown feathers and softly cried….'well, maybe not…'

Then determined, the sparrow fluttered her wings and forcibly proclaimed, 'then I want to be seen as intelligent and smart!'

The fox turned over where he was laying on the ground,

Stretched out his paws to the sky….

He turned back to the sparrow and said with a sigh,

'You mean like the raven or crow?'

'Well no,' said the sparrow, her beak pointing low.

'Ah ha!' claimed the sparrow then what about proud?'

What if I were thought of above the general crowd?'

The fox yawned getting tired and twitched his red tail; he turned to the sparrow and with an exhale, 'you mean like the hawk or owl so wise?' 'Tell me my friend when you look in my eyes, do you see me as a wolf or a hound?' 'Do you think I'm as sly as a rat or a cat?' 'I am me and you are beautiful you ......and my friend it is winter and here we both are; enduring the hardships of the season thus far.' 'No one can do what the two of us can.' 'We are ......you and I...... the very best friends.' 'Not afraid of the trials and life's turning bends; we are strengthened by hardships and blessed by rewards; of life when it's full, warm and tranquil, yet don't run when the cold of loneliness bites at our heal.'

'So my dear little sparrow you are precious to me and I "cherish" you more than life's frivolity.'

The sparrow thought, then tilted her head, flapped her brown wings and quiet loudly said.... 'Then nothing in life is more important than that!'

'The love of a friend who endures to the end, through the rest of our lives we'll be together, even when we find ourselves living through our lows and our highs.'

And with that they both trailed away quiet content, knowing their friendship would never relent.

-signed me

It felt good. I knew that it was not a masterpiece yet it was my plea for acceptance. I wanted a friend to reassure me that I did not have to prove myself. That I would just be accepted for who I was and what I could offer in a relationship by just being me.

This is how I looked at my son. At times we had gone through little trials but I tried to learn from them and teach him something too. Not destroy who he was over them but build him up. I remember an incident when he was 13.

I had come home from a 12 hour shift at the hospital and met a timid young man at the door.

Lifting a suspicious eye brow I greeted him.

"Hello Jason, how was your day?" I took my work shoes off never looking away from him. Something was up, he was not himself.

He nervously looked over at our antique standing lamp, near the living room wall that entered into the hallway to the bedrooms. "Fine mom, how was your day?" He looked back quickly at me and smiled.

"Good. My day was good." I too looked quickly at the lamp then back at him. "Anything interesting that has happened today?" I asked. "Did you do your homework, and what did you have for dinner?" I started to walk into the kitchen to get myself a drink of juice.

On my days off work I would make a bunch of TV dinners and freeze them for when I couldn't be home to cook for him. Or, he would just make himself a sandwich or soup.

"Yes I did my homework, I ate some BBQ chicken with mashed potatoes; and yes I had some vegetables with it." He genuinely smiled thinking he would beat me to the next common question I would ask him.

"You are too awesome!" I laughed and looking around the kitchen noticed that he had cleaned up after himself too. "And thank you for cleaning the kitchen! You did a great job!" After pouring myself some apple juice from the fridge, I went to the table to sit down so I could hear more about his day before we said good night to one another.

"Mom….." He joined me at the table and with resignation in his voice began sharing with me something that he didn't really want to.

"Mom ……I broke the lamp." There he said it and he looked relieved but kept going. "I didn't mean to. I was running through the house and knocked into it. It fell over and the glass broke. I tried to put it back together because it only broke in three pieces. I wasn't going to tell you and just let you find out on your own one day, but I know that you don't like dishonesty." He sat there staring at the table waiting for his sentence of torture to come crashing down upon him.

I got up from the table and walked into the living room to look at the lamp. Sure enough it was broken, barely placed together yet put back together in a way that I would not have noticed. 'hm, interesting' I thought as I took the pieces and brought them back into the kitchen to place them on the table.

"Well, I am really happy that you told me the truth. There is no reprimand for telling me the truth Jason, thank you for that." I was truly pleased with him.

He was now showing complete relief at this point.

"However…." I continued, "There are natural consequences that have to be addressed."

He waited silently.

"Someone has to buy a new lamp shade. It is probably going to cost around $50 to $100 dollars so, I will add a couple more chores on the 'chores list'. I will raise the amount that each chore is worth and on my next day off we will go and you can buy a new lamp shade for me from your earned allowance."

The 'chore list' I spoke of was a way I thought I could teach my son that nothing in life is free so neither will I just give him an allowance just because he was my son. I had put all the possible little chores around the house which included things like ....making his bed, doing the dishes, sweeping, cleaning his room, vacuuming, dusting, watering plants, gathering the garbage, taking the garbage out on garbage day, mowing the grass, pulling weeds in the flower garden, raking the grass and washing the car. I never made him do any of it. They all had a dollar value to them. He was the one that chose how much money he wanted for his allowance on Friday and he did chores to match that amount. Sometimes he would do them twice which made me laugh when he brought me 'the bill'.

"I will pay for half of the cost and also the taxes. We will also look for one that is maybe not as expensive as this one was; how does that sound?"

He jumped up from the table and ran to where I was sitting across from him, and gave me a hug knowing that he would end up having a normal allowance on Friday if he put his mind to it and also be able to afford to pay half for a new lamp shade.

"That sounds fair mom!"

"Then the issue is settled....and again Jason....thank you for being honest with me. I value that very much in you, thank you!"

Value. Everyone has value. This part of a character needs to be built up, not torn down. If you take this down in a person, then what can they give you, or themselves?

Jason's value as a person has been torn apart by his dad and his dad's family. So has mine. What good are we now? Jason was a hurting young man now, and not sure which direction he is going. This was so unlike who he used to be. I tried to show Jason that he is still an incredible person. Yet having myself worth and character shredded also; left me with a hole in my heart probably as big as the bleeding one that was now in his.

Another thing I did at this point in the emptiness of my life was painting. Each painting meant something to me. They spoke of hope in a dark time. I placed light in each one representing hope. Sometimes the light came from a candle, other times it came from a hidden source, sometimes from the moon or the sun just about to rise. Always hope.

I even started getting requests for paintings including a model asking for her portrait to be painted. I entertained the thought of doing this for a living, but it was just that.....a thought.

I continued to write.

SCRIBBLINGS....

Twisted wind, winding maze

Twirling round a fogy haze

Circling questions, crying rage

Unencumbered hurtful days

Thoughtful moments, sunshine spent

Lost in what those words all meant

Hopeful intentions, wishing again

Wondering ......had I gone insane

125

Quiet prayers, whispered aloud
    Voice denied, don't be proud
Waiting still, holding strong
    I won't let this go too long
'Nothing ventured, nothing gained'
    I'll jump in....it hasn't waned
Twisted wind, questions role
    God help my helpless soul!
Opened answers, clearer air
    We would make an awesome pair
Breathing easy, I now see
    Some of what we should be
Closing eyelids, stretching mind
    Pushing unease to unwind
Tossing pennies, wishes made
    Wanting all are dues be paid
Fathers blessings, from the throne
    Will this be (God) my new home?
Gift of heaven, in a son
    Finally now has true love won?
-signed me

    This was a wonderful way to express myself. I knew what everything meant. If someone cares to know me better they would really look to understand what I wrote. If they did not care to understand me, then they would not look to understand. Simple.

    Then another story.

THE ICE RINK

It's an ice rink and it is all hers.

Her little head nervously turned this way and that way.

Her eyes tried to peer through the darkness, grabbing desperately at the red light from the rising sun.

Still she could see and hear no sounds.

It's clear; she thought.

Taking one more almost scared look around, she opened her little wings and glided down to the frozen fountain with hardly a sound.

Slipping slightly at first, she regained her balance and gently started pushing herself around.

There was a slight winter breeze that caressed the snow drifts on either side of the fountain.

The clean, coolness of the air wafting around her was like perfume sent from heaven just for her.

Light grew wider as if the sun itself was yawning tiredness away, to begin its days work.

Stretching her wings out, she picked up speed and swung around in circles on her private ice rink.

She heard a friend waking in a distant tree calling to others, getting ready a search party to look for food.

She turned and attempted a little jump fluttering her wings to the left.

The snow had shed its grey cover of darkness now and sparkled a million colors through its hidden diamonds.

Free form fear for a moment, all worries slipped away and an almost giddiness flowed in her veins.

She was now swirling and twirling in-between graceful jumps on her ice rink, carefree and happy.

Then she turned and fear slapped her in the face, stopping her movements and ripping her joy away.

Where did he come from?!

Why had she not heard his approach?

The cold slit, yellow eyes squinted at her, reminding her of immediate death.

"God I am your sparrow!' she cried out, 'forgive me for not keeping watch, help!'

Death pounced, her wings spread; and she felt herself being lifted into the safe hands of God.

-signed me

This was all I had to keep my mind company. My son was not living in the house right now, my husband was away from me as much as he could be and when he was home he did not talk to me. He was either, on his computer, watching TV or downstairs. He didn't need to be with me. I wasn't worth his attention or time.

I wrote him a poem one day…..

THE DOG

I wait for you patiently; my master of the home.

I run from the window to the door, I'm all alone.

When I hear your car come home, I wage my little tail.

I want to see if your happy with me, I do not want to fail.

You walk into the house and ignore me, I'm in your way.

I haven't seen you for so long, yet you have nothing to say.

I jump around quietly, because with you I found.

You don't like it when I speak to you, so see I make no sound.

You hate it when I look to you to give me some attention.

If you have any interest in me, of this you make no mention.

I know the rules you give me, do not speak until spoken too.

And don't ask questions about anything you do.

But now the loneliness squeezes joyfulness out.

How can I get you to notice, my aching heart pout.

You hate my bark

You hate my ways

You hate my shape
I'm in a haze
You hate my color
You hate my eyes
You hate that to me
You have any ties
I wonder if there is anything that I could do for you.
to make the statement 'I'm glad I'm with you' true.
-signed me

I read some of my poems to him. Mack just said 'nice', and continued what he was doing.

12

Taking a Stand

I finally got a job. 'This will do it,' I thought. This will make my husband like me more. I got a job at a hospital without taking 'the test'.

I struggled to get to work and back, I either had to rely on Mack's parents, or him when he was available or the bus if I had some tickets. This was not a comfortable position to be in. I was getting stressed from being treated like a burden. Obviously the job was not changing anything in any one's eyes about me, because of 'that fact' the job was not pleasurable.

I loved that I was working and the fast pace and full work load was a blessing to my mind. Yet, I hated the struggle with the fact that I never seemed to have any money to eat lunch. The fact that I struggled with the language, struggled with the 'how do I get to and from work' situation. Not to mention that Mack would yell and scream at me all the way to work if he had to talk to me at all while we were in the car together. He said I made him miserable and showed it every day and night. Sometimes I would be walking into the hospital in tears to start my day because of the names he would call me before he dropped me off. He always had a reason to be mad at me. I just gave him too many reasons; it was always my fault that he was mad at me.

He had the right to yell at me if he had a headache. If he was tired. If he was hungry. If I did not appreciate everything that he did for me. He had the right to yell at me if I did not agree with his way of thinking. If I didn't like one of his shows. If I didn't want to go to his parents place for supper. He had a right to call me names if I asked him questions about his day. Or if he heard me asking Jason about his day, he would be mad because he said that I cared about Jason more than I cared for him. He would have an obligation to get mad at me if I didn't put something back where he could find it or hang something up or clean something almost before I was finished using it or doing what I was doing. Not only did I deserve this treatment from him but also his parents, family, friends or anyone else that gave me disrespect. I always deserved it.

So, I started bringing to his attention every woman that he showed interest or respect too. If he honestly could not treat me better than a stranger than he should try to date or introduce himself to a woman that he does respect and enjoy looking at and being with.

There was nothing I was doing or could do to change anything. So could I really make matters worse?

I demanded that my son move back home. Or I would move out. Amazingly; Jason came home.

And…………………..…Mack took me on a vacation.

We went to Florida to visit one of his cousins. By the time we got there I was sick of the silence. There had been nothing fun about the trip. Nothing shared between us, nothing we would be able to take pictures of or talk about later. He talked endlessly with his cousin and his cousin's wife. One day his cousins' wife took us to a beach. We stopped for a drink after Mack went for a swim. He still just talked to her. Not me. At one point a young, tall, blonde waitress came over asking us if we wanted another drink. I asked Mack, who was not looking at me; and without turning told me firmly 'no'. So, I told the waitress no. I then left to use the washroom and when I returned I noticed that Mack had another drink in front of him. What was wrong! He had to talk to the waitress and ask for a drink himself. He didn't want it to have gone through me? I looked at the tall, slim, young, blond waitress. He had to order from her himself. Why can't he treat me the same way he treated strangers!

"I thought you didn't want anything else to drink?" I queried.

"What the fuck is the problem!" he responded angrily, "I changed my mind!" He looked at his cousins' wife as if she should notice the horrible person he married. "There is no SIN in changing my mind....fuck!"

'No Mack,' I thought to myself. 'There is no SIN in changing your mind but did you? Or did you hate the thought of having to tell your drink order to me instead of you talking to the cute young waitress yourself?'

As we left the beach I was walking alone behind Mack and his cousins' wife. He couldn't walk with someone that pissed him off so much.

After a couple days we left there to go to Disney World.

We stayed at a hotel and went to one of the different parks for three days in a row. I felt like he wanted to be there and enjoy himself. Just not with me.

He was with me but he wasn't with me at the same time.

I wanted him to communicate with me the same way he would talk with others.

All of the questions I asked him were met with a yes or no response from him. We kept to statements with each other rather than conversation. 'Do you want to go on this ride?' 'It's hot out.' 'I don't want to wait in this long of a line up, let's go to a different ride.' 'Okay...... yes...... no.'

On our last evening in one of the parks before we went back to the hotel, he had a long easy conversation with a young waitress.

She liked his accent and wanted to know where he was from. Well, he told her where he was from how long he lived there, what he was doing there in Florida and much more.

My resentment built up. Why was he so pleased to converse with a complete stranger so easily and take his time patiently explaining things and answering question from her? Why does he continually refuse to talk to me like that! I kept silent.

By the time we got back to the hotel, he turned the TV on and then after an hour without talking to me; went to sleep.

Rejection stabbed at my heart all night. How can I make myself interesting enough to him that he would want to spend time with me? Not just be in the same room or location but actually spend time with me? I didn't sleep almost all night.

By the time morning came he woke up still not saying anything to me.

I exploded.

"Why can't you talk to me?" I asked in complete frustration.

"I don't know what you're talking about!" He yelled back.

"I want you to talk to me like you did with your cousins or that waitress last night!"

That was it. He poured out his rage on me. "You fucking jealous bitch!!!!" "You can go fuck yourself!!!!" He started throwing things around the hotel, calling me names and swearing at me. He threw everything that was his into his suitcase and slammed the door to the hotel; leaving me alone after screaming at me the whole time it took for him to pack his things.

I sat in silence. The seconds turned into minutes, and then turned into an hour. I got up and packed my bags. I had no money, no cell phone that could be used and no one to phone anyway.

I didn't know how I was going to get back to Montréal from Florida. I no longer knew anything.

Why didn't I just let him treat me like a nothing? Why did I have to keep asking him to treat me like he does everyone else? This had nothing to do with being jealous. This had everything to do with the fact that he was my husband and was supposed to be my 'best friend'. Not everyone else's best friend. I was not supposed to be treated like an unwanted dog. I was not supposed to 'just keep quiet' and let him treat me like this. But....I didn't know how to stop him from hating me and what I was doing was making everything worse.

He showed me that he had no problem with humiliating me in public. Like when he would yell at me in a restaurant or gas station.

I had no choice. If he was still here, I would have to ask him for a ride back to Canada. I had no choice.

I took my bag and wheeled it down to the hotel's restaurant. There he was, sitting at a table finishing a cup of coffee and reading a newspaper. He apparently finished his breakfast already because there was an empty plate beside him on the table.

The restaurant was empty except two young women that were sitting at the table next to him. Did he sit down first and the women sat close to him, or did they sit first and he wanted to sit close to them? Only two tables being used in the whole place and the occupants had to be sitting right beside each other. Well, his parents were right, he was a good looking man and women wanted him. I just wish he would make up his mind as to what he wanted.

I opened the door and looked at him. Would he wave me in or yell at me to go screw myself? He did neither. He looked up and then with no emotion turned back to reading his paper. I was nothing to him.

I closed the door and sat on the steps of the restaurant with my bag. He didn't want me to be with him right now. I would have to wait until he came out to see if I could get a ride with him.

I waited there for almost another half hour before he came out. He swung the door wide, gave me a disgusted look and walked away to use the rest room in the hotel lobby. I got up and walked over to the men's washroom door with my bag, and waited there.

He came out and without saying a word walked past me to the car parking lot where his car was. I followed him like a dog. He got into his car, put on his seat belt and started the car. He put it in reverse then rolled his window down and yelled at me to 'get the fuck into the car'.

The trip back was just as horribly lonely as the trip down. After two days of being with someone that just did not want to be with me, we had another 'fight'.

We were almost three hours away from the Canadian border and he threw the GPS at me and told me to read it. It was messing up and the arrow was not on any of the roads.

"We just have to stay on this highway; it will take us to the border." I said.

"READ IT TO ME!" he yelled. "LOOK AT IT LIKE A MAP!"

"It is not telling us to turn anywhere; we are on a highway Mack. I don't think we need it anymore." I didn't see any reason to try to read a GPS that was not working right when we were almost at the Canadian border and could be home in a couple hours after crossing it.

"YOU STUPID BITCH!" "YOU ARE THE STUPIDIST PERSON I HAVE EVER MET IN MY LIFE!" "I HAVE NEVER MET ANYONE STUPIDER THAN YOU IN ALL MY LIFE!"

Mack was punching his car door and rage filled him as he spouted out how stupid I was. He began once again to drive madly and did not stop yelling at me for three hours. I know it was this long because he didn't stop until we got to the border. That was three hours after he asked me to read his GPS.

Obviously we made it without having to use the GPS.

Obviously I was not going to point that out to him right now.

After we crossed the border and started picking up speed to merge back on the highway, a young girl cut him off. He turned in her direction in anger.

He saw that it was a lovely young girl behind the wheel.

He turned back to his driving and let her go ahead of him without another word.

We made it home and he went straight into his parents' house to have a couple drinks with them and probably complain about me.

Jason was in the apartment when I opened the door.

"How was your trip?" he asked with a hopeful expression.

"Don't ask Jason," I stated; "and ………….I would pretend you are sleeping when your dad comes up from downstairs or he is going to find something to get mad at you for too."

Jason came over to me and gave me a hug.

"How long are you going to live like this mom?" my heart ripped open further when I heard the anguish in his voice. He was torn between not being able to protect himself from his dad and not being able to protect me from Mack either.

"Not long Jason." I tried to reassure him. We both went to our rooms. Mack never came back up the stairs until he was drunk and probably ran out of things to complain about over the trip he had just come back from with me.

He didn't talk to me when he came into the bedroom, threw his clothes off and went right to sleep.

I went back to work two days later and completely lost my ability to concentrate on anything.

Jason tried to kill himself with alcohol a week later. I tried to stay with him as much as I could. I tried to talk to him and be with him and work with him to not let his dad destroy him like this.

It was the wounded trying to lead the wounded.

Mack was taking me to Wal-Mart to pick up a couch/bed for Jason. He would need something to sleep on if he were to move out, I told Mack. So he agreed to buy him one.

As we were driving down a crowded street, we had to slow the car a little to go around a cyclist that was also going around a parked car. There was no room for any of us to move due to the oncoming traffic, which was just as crowded as we were on this street.

I winced as we went around the cyclist, quickly praying he didn't fall and that we didn't hit him.

I broke the silence of the ride.

"Oh man that scares me to have to drive around a cyclist on such a small busy road." I mentioned, "If I were biking on a road like this I would be using the sidewalk very slowly."

Wrong thing to say. Mack loved to ride his bike.

Once again, I found myself being yelled at and being called names and watching as Mack punched the inside of his car and drive angrily the rest of the way to Wal-Mart. We were about 20 minutes from the store when I mistakenly made that comment. By the time we arrived in the parking lot and Mack swore his last curse at me; I was shattered. I was holding my head and leaning into the dash crying.

He turned the ignition off and turning to me he said.........."well? You coming?"

I looked up at him with insane amazement. My eyes and face were still full of tears. My nose was running so I reached for a Kleenex and blew it. Then, bracing myself for more; I stood my ground.

"I am not going into that store now." I stated quietly. "I am devastated, hurt and would not be able to concentrate." I sucked my breath in as he started showing signs of anger again, and looking at him I finished...."I will not walk around Wal-Mart, looking like a depressed woman."

He drove back home racing through the streets in anger.

I marveled, 'he calls me crazy; yet he is capable of exploding like this in absolute rage then want to walk around a store as if nothing was wrong!'

What is crazier......the one full of irrational anger or the one trying to figure the angry one out?

After a couple more weeks of working......I quit my job. I was unable to 'save' any money from working there any way. I was unable to keep my depression from my job. I was unable to help my son.

So, one day when Mack came home from work, I was sitting at the kitchen table waiting for him.

"We need to talk." I stated flatly.

"What the fuck now!" he retorted, "I am not in the mood!"

"I am going to go back to BC with or without you Mack." I actually saw him scoff before I continued.

"I will be taking what I can and leaving in June." I never moved or changed my tone. "I will be leaving with Jason back to BC this June."

It was a couple months away. I needed time to see if Jason or I could get some money for the trip back to BC. We were going to leave this province for good! I was a 'horrible' wife that just made him 'miserable' and that he 'hated to talk to' or 'do anything' with. I was the most 'boring slut' he knew, so; I think it is time I truly give him his freedom from such a rotten 'bitch' like me.

Mack stared at me for a long time.

I didn't move.

He walked towards the door to leave the apartment. Stopped at the open front door before closing it hard behind him and made just as bold a statement back to me.

"Then I am going with you!"

13

Another Move

Mack was busy with his job. He was out of his 'home office' every day from Monday to Friday. He had also taken time off to go through an interview process with a new company in the West. A new company that he had just been hired to work for. The company was primarily based out of the states yet had several major offices in Canada. They flew him to Seattle providing him with the best of accommodations and to Edmonton twice. They picked him up in limousines and fed him in fine restaurants. He was really excited about his new job and everything that came with it. He never talked to me about the new job. We never talked about the move together. We never planned about starting our lives over in a new place.

We never talked. I only heard him talking to people on the phone. He went over details and all the planning of his new job with his 'family' (which did not include Jason or I), soon to be co-workers and employer. Not with me.

I tried to talk to him about finding a place with me via the internet. His reply was frustration that I would bother him about this boring stuff. "You could do that' he stated frankly to me. I was only to let him know when I found a place.

I wondered about moving with him, he showed no interest in sharing any part of the move with me. He had quit his job and got a more exciting one that still did not seem to include me in any form.

I tried to ask him to help me pack. To which he replied that he was too busy and he "trusted me" to take care of that.

My determination to get out of this province and away from his parents grew stronger every day. So I pushed myself to make sure everything in regards to organizing a move across Canada would go smoothly.

I was getting exhausted dealing with his parents and their problems. Like I didn't have enough of my own problems in my marriage to their son? His dad would come up to bring us our mail and ask us the same question every 30 minutes of the day. Sometimes he unlocked our door and came in at night. He would wake us up saying that I was downstairs just now calling to him. He would want to know where we had put something. He would be looking for his wife, which after all these years had just walked out on him.

Her leaving him was not a surprise to me after having to listen to countless lectures by them over the years I had lived above (or 'with') them. I learned how he thought and wondered in amazement that people with such a distorted view on life managed to hold a marriage together. Mack's dad treated his wife like Mack treated me. Both father and son thought anything other than what they deemed right or wrong was quite simply wrong and their opinions were in fact the only right and wrong in the universe. If you didn't agree with them completely you would need to hire a lawyer, bring engineered blue prints or secure a team of wise men to prove them wrong. Or just simply pull it up on the all knowledgable internet. No way on this side of heaven could you just say….'well it's what I believe' or 'that is how I do it'. Never ever, ever would that statement be approved. You even had to give detailed reason as to why you had folded a chip bag differently. You couldn't just 'do it'; you had to explain why if it was different from what they were doing.

Yes they both thought the exact same way, almost in every subject and area of life. The bizarre thing about the two of them was….they couldn't be in the same room with each other without having an argument. That is if they had to talk to one another. That's when other people came into play. Like when I was with them then I was the one that had to talk to his dad and keep him 'entertained'.

One lecture I received from them was after Mack had gone downstairs drinking with them and yelling and crying to them about what a jealous woman I was. Mack's dad had called me downstairs and began telling me that 'his son was so good looking that it was only natural that other women wanted him.' 'I just had to live with the fact that I married such an amazingly good looking man.' He then gave me an example of what a 'normal' marriage was all about using a past incident with him and his wife.

He said....'one day at a staff party I was dancing with this beautiful woman I worked with. I had a huge hard on! She was touching me and wanted to love me, then my wife came in-between us and pushed the woman away yelling at her to get her own husband.' He seemed so proud of this, and said to me, but I was a beautiful man to her (meaning his co-worker).'

I seethed at Mack over this insane lecture I had gotten later that day when I saw him. I told him what I thought of that advice after hearing that he agreed with it. I quite simply and emphatically stated that he will not get that type of response from me!

"It is not MY job to stop a woman from hitting on you or from you hitting on another woman!" I could barely control myself at this point. I wanted him to understand a solid truth about our union! "If you want another woman I CAN NOT STOP YOU! It is YOUR job to let other women know that you are married and no longer available!" I was almost shaking with determination to get my point across (the lecture I had to endure again was par with all the other ones by taking around two hours.)"I WILL NOT INTERFERE WITH YOU AND ANOTHER WOMAN, EVER!" I made my final statement hopefully

143

perfectly clear. "THAT IS YOUR JOB JUST LIKE IT IS MY JOB TO MAKE IT CLEAR TO OTHER MEN THAT I AM NOT AVAILABLE OR WILLING TO 'BE ENTERTAINED' BY THEM!"

Mack didn't agree. He didn't like the fact that I would not jump in and 'fight' for my man. I knew that he didn't get that I should not have to fight for him. We should both be responsible to stay 'faithful' to one another on our own. It was unrealistic to think otherwise. I would not be able to follow him around trying to stop the women from pursuing him. And yes! I get it! HE IS BEAUTIFUL AND IT IS ONLY NATURAL FOR HIM TO NOTICE BEAUTIFUL WOMEN AND FOR THEM TO NOTICE HIM!

"Get that in your head!" "Get that in your head!" "GET THAT IN YOUR HEAD!"

With every lecture I got from Mack he would repeat that angrily to me. Yelling it at me. In every argument or I mean every 'subject' we 'talked' about. Almost daily I heard those words............."GET THAT IN YOUR HEAD!" He would sometimes push his fingers into his temples or bang the top of his head to emphasize the words.

'Yes!' I get it; I get it, I GET IT!'

I get how you see me. I get how you think about me. I get the names that you call me. I get that I am nothing of importance to you. Not as important to him as his mom, or his sister or ….yes….even his dad.

One evening I came home from working late and as soon as I entered our place I got blasted. He was drunk and spent the whole evening with his parents and sister down in their parents place. Without even saying hello to me or anything at all, he started yelling and spitting in my face that…"he was going to be there for his sister anytime she wanted him so fuck me. He would be

144

there for his sister always so fuck Jason." He yelled more profanities at me before going to bed.

I turned on my heals and went back downstairs into his parents place without knocking and met his mother near the entrance.

"What happened tonight!?" I fumed. "I just walk into the house after being gone all day and I get yelled at by your son telling me he is going to be there for his sister so "FUCK ME AND FUCK JASON! I have never said or done anything wrong in regards to his sister! What in the world happened tonight that made me an evil person tonight? I wasn't even here!"

His mommy just looked at me with innocent eyes and said..."I don't know Tammy."

She bloody well knew! She knew that after getting stinking drunk, they were all probably crying on each other's shoulders about their problems and drunkenly decided that all the problems in this family's life were because of me.

I could see that Mack's sister was probably upset with him for not being there for her since she was going through a not so nice break up with her long time boyfriend, and I would almost guarantee that that is when the bitch wife came into the conversations. He had to have an excuse as to why he wasn't there for her and it could not be because he just didn't care to get involved and help his sister out.

None of them could be responsible human beings. There always had to be someone that they needed to blame for who they were and how they acted, and that person was apparently me tonight and who knows how many other nights before this one.

Mack could not say that "I must have done something to piss him off" or "I must have said something to piss him off" as he ALWAYS does after he freaks out on me for sometimes NO REASON WHAT—SO—EVER!!!!!

I was exhausted mentally. I had to get away from them! I could not think if I had to get away from Mack too at this point. I just wanted away from Mack's family before I lost myself completely.

In between getting the move organized and a place ready for us to move to; I had to take his dad to doctor appointments. His mom was not there anymore and Mack was 'just too busy' and so apparently was his sister.

On one of Mack's weekends that he could have helped me with our move; his mom phoned and asked him to help her with her move.

He didn't hesitate to go, and he was gone all day long. (Interesting that he never helped with his dads' move, even though mind wise; his dad needed the most help.)

The depths of emotions were playing havoc with my mind and heart. 'Of course his mom's move is much, much, much more important than helping your wife with YOURS!' I screamed in my mind at him.

'Keep it together Tammy,' I would console myself; 'this is your ticket out of this province and away from his family.'

Maybe once he is away from his family he will treat me better. We could maybe start to lean on each other for support like a married couple should. Leaning on mommy should end after you are married ......shouldn't it? Maybe moving to the West will show him 'why' women in the east want a man from the West and not one of their own French men for husbands because the West has morals!

He never 'leaned' on me, or came to me for support of any kind. Observing him with his mother though I had an idea that maybe what he was looking for was another mommy that would agree and empathize with everything he said or did. I never even did that for my own son.

146

Although, Mack and his family had put me in a position of complete protective defense after we moved here.

Yes, Mack was way too busy to help me with the move. He was always busy and away from the house.

He never told me what he did when he left the house. Although on one occasion after he came home a little later than he usually did, I asked him how his day went.

I noticed that he had left his computer, notebook and everything else that he usually left the house with at home that day. I was interested in his answer.

"I had lunch with a client and then went to the office and worked all day finishing up emails and closing accounts!" he almost yelled this at me, completely irritated that I would ask him once again anything about his day away from me.

"You must have had a lot of work to do on your computer then," I said softly, almost empathetically. "You are late coming home." I looked away from him casually beginning to show interest in some papers from the movers that were in front of me on the table. "I trust your computer didn't give you any troubles today with opening files then?" As he stated it had to me in the past.

He didn't even hesitate in his response. "No, I did a lot of work today and it was fucking boring."

I couldn't wait to move.

Jason was all packed and helped me when ever his dad was not around which was indeed quite often.

Mack came home and told me that he would have to 'let' Jason and I drive his car across Canada. It would be cheaper than having the movers haul it there. He would give me $1000 to make the move. (This way, he wouldn't have to pay for us to fly either.) That was to include gas, food, and 'if' we needed to stop anywhere to sleep, then a hotel too. He also informed me that he would not be with

147

us because his new employer was going to send him to Chicago for a two week training session for his new job.

(Ah yes, I thought, who wouldn't want to ride in limousines, eat in fine restaurants and stay in luxury hotels for two weeks instead of move your family?)

"Your employer gave you two dates for that training in Chicago, if you took the second date a couple weeks after this one then you would be able to be with us for this move?" Was I really asking him to make us a priority in his life? I knew what he was going to say before he said it and even how he would respond to my query before he opened his mouth.

"I NEED TO EARN SOME MONEY HERE! THIS MOVE IS NOT CHEAP!" Mack commenced in a rampage of how DARE I even suggest such a stupid thing!

Chicago (or anything for that matter) was way more exciting and desirable than being with me. 'I get it!'

I was not going to remind him that his new employer was going to reimburse him for the major part of the cost of the move. He knew that information, if he really wanted to be a supportive family member, he would want to do this move with us. So at the end of the day (so to speak) it would not be as big a cost as if we had to do it on our own. Would it really bring him to the brink of bankruptcy if he were to be with me? Apparently yes. He was not willing to make that kind of sacrifice.

I listened to him for almost 20 minutes telling me what an ungrateful bitch I was before he stormed out of the house got into his car and drove off to who knows where.

'Tammy,' I chided myself; 'how could you be so heartless and ask such a thing from your husband?'

I sat back in my chair at the table and looked vacantly at the fridge. There was a ripped and crumpled photo of me in a broken fridge magnet that I had been given from a friend of mine. It was a little going away /

wedding gift when I left Kelowna. Mack was mad at me one day and vengefully destroyed my picture. He destroyed my image. ....

That thought numbed my mind.

His anger numbed my heart.

The names he called me numbed my soul.

I got up like an empty robot. Like an empty human being. Someone had flipped the switch off on 'Tammy'. I walked over to the fridge, reached for my broken image, stared at it for a moment not knowing what I should be thinking, or why I would want this piece of garbage anymore. Almost without breathing, I walked over to the kitchen garbage bin that was hidden under the sink and tossed the photo and frame into it. I stood there for what seemed like an hour not moving. Just standing there and staring down at the garbage bin. 'I should be wary of this.' Psychologically this vehement act of his towards an image of my face should be screaming something to me.' Yet, my mind wasn't working right now, just like my heart.

Freedom at last.

A week later, I watched the moving truck pull out of the driveway. Jason and I got into Mack's car, put our seatbelts on and I turned the key in the ignition.

I pulled out of the driveway. Jason and I never spoke a word. It was almost as if we were both holding our breaths.

It had been two days since I spoke to Mack. Why would he phone to enquire if the movers had came or if Jason or I was alright? He was in Chicago. We could take care of ourselves. He didn't have to care how we were. Why would he call or text? He was with his new 'friends'.

I pulled out onto the freeway leaving the city. It was already getting dark and the city lights were reflecting off of the front of the car hood as we sped along with the rest of the traffic.

Finally; after driving for over an hour, we were out of the city.

Sobbing broke the silence. My hands gripped the steering wheel and my whole body shook with such a deep sorrowful sobbing, that it became hard to concentrate on my driving. I struggled to see through my tears out the window and into the night.

"Mom!" Jason put his hand on my shoulder, "are you okay?"

I looked at him for a second and then turned my attention back to the road.

"We are out of there!" I cried more softly now. "We are out of there!" I almost could not believe it! "We will never have to go back Jason!" I spoke so softly that I thought for a moment that he hadn't heard me.

"We never will mom." He gripped my shoulder and his voice sounded so solid and unbendable. "It is over."

I didn't know what laid ahead for either one of us. Jason was going to concentrate on getting a job that would enable him to live on his own. After all, he reminded me, that 'dad' was moving with us. He no longer wanted to be under his dad's control. Under his dad's bizarre split personality and perfectionism.

My dad was enraged with Mack. I finally broke down and cried to him on the phone one day about how my life with Mack was really going. He was livid and hated himself for 'giving me to such an ungrateful man.' He couldn't understand why Mack was not able to see how blessed he was for the opportunity to have Jason and I in his life. He was determined to talk to Jason after that phone call as often as he could to let him know what a great kid he was. My dad begged Jason to work on not letting how Mack was treating him or how Mack was talking to or about him, to interfere with knowing who he truly was. My dad was so proud of his grandson. He would ask in unbelief why he (Mack) wasn't 'tickled up the ass' at having a son that was not into drugs or partying like so many of his peers. He could not believe that he wasn't thankful that he had a son that would forgive and love him as much as Jason had when Mack first came back into our lives. My dad didn't understand why Mack did the things he did, that is until he flew down to see how things were going for himself, and my dad met Mack's dad. After that, my dad no longer asked why Mack was the way he was. Instead he would tell me that if I left Mack he would support me 100% (That meant emotional support because my dad was on a small pension and he started to wish that he had more money to just come down and get me out of there). He also said that he loved me so much that if I decided to stay with Mack and try to work on our marriage then he would support that also. My dad did his best to be impartial when he was speaking to Mack on the phone. He was afraid that he may make Mack mad and that because of that it would be harder on Jason and I. My dad was my hero! I loved him so much. When I was little I thought that I wanted to marry someone just like my dad.

Boy did I ever marry the opposite of my dad.

My dad left Montréal disgusted with some of the stuff he heard and seen. But he thanked Mack never the less for the opportunity to come down for a visit and see where his daughter was living. On the phone to me once he was home he told me that Mack's dad asked him if he wanted to sleep with his wife.

"Tammy! You have to tell me that he was joking! Why would he degrade her so badly?" my dad asked incredibly.

"I honestly don't know how to answer that dad." I replied. "One of the reasons that his wife is separating from him over is the fact that he had his 14 year old niece 'play with him'." I gave him a little more detail and my dad just about puked on the other end of the phone.

"Tammy you have to get away from them!" He sounded desperate to get me out of there and closer to him. Closer to BC.

"I am working on it dad." I promised him.

My dad wanted me to leave Mack, he knew there was someone out there that would respect, protect and love me. Never the less as long as I chose to stay with Mack, my dad would respect that he was my husband. He also felt betrayed by him in the sense that after the wedding, my dad asked Mack to promise him that he would take care of me and Jason. My dad has since seen that the only way Mack was 'taking care' of us was keeping a roof over our heads. There was no love or respect shown us. Mack was very clear that his 'family' (meaning mom, dad and sister would always come before us). My dad stated simply.....''that wasn't a man."

By the time we had driven across the Ontario border both Jason and I were fighting sleep. It had been a long day that began with a horrible sleep the night before as we both tried to curl up on a cold floor in between boxes. During that awful night every time I had a thought about Mack and the fact that he hadn't called us or the fact that I knew he had a full stomach from fine food and a warm bed to sleep in; built resentment in me. It was the epitome of selfishness. It was his 'I am OK and don't care if you are' attitude that I loathed. All it would have taken from him to build in me love and not resentment was one phone call from him.

'Tammy, how are you doing?' or 'Tammy I hope everything is going well with you and the move,' or 'Tammy, I miss you and wish I was there to help you move.' ....Yah, in my dreams.

One phone call is all it would take from him to re-create love. One phone call to let me know he cared was all I would have needed to love him back.

He could not be bothered. He never phoned.

Jason and I arrived at a little hotel outside of Ottawa and after paying for one night, went to bed hungry and exhausted.

The next morning I looked at what I had left, calculated what it was going to cost to go the rest of the way then turned to Jason with a smile and said...."Well, good news!" "We are going to be able to afford McDonalds all the way across Canada two times each day."

"At least it will be food mom." He laughed.

That night we were closer to the border of Manitoba and out of anger I text Mack.

'By the way....just to let you know....we are still alive....and ....gee.....I hope you are having a great time!'

'What the fuck is your problem now! I am busy WORKING. I am not having any FUN!'

I looked at Jason. "Can you feel how much he misses me? Poor man! Can you imagine just starting a new job and already his new employer must be pinning him down and torturing him! Yah, I am absolutely positive he is having absolutely no fun ....at......ALL!"

"I better leave him to enjoy the rest of his night with people he actually likes being with. He must truly think I am an absolute idiot," I paused, "wait a minute....am I one for putting up with this treatment?"

Jason had a pained expression pass over his face and without saying a word placed his hand on mine over the clutch and stared out the front window.

A couple nights later when I tried to phone him at 10:30 at night, there was a woman's voice in the background and apparently he was still up and sitting in a lounge drinking.

Interesting.

I was completely trained over the past two years that I needed to go to bed no later than 10 o'clock. At which time ...."I WAS NOT ALLOWED TO TALK!!!!!!!!!!!"

He completely freaked out on me. Over the phone he told me there were only MEN at this workshop. Yelling at me what a 'jealous, insane, paranoid, bitch/slut I was'. He stood his ground on that fact (only men), that is until I seen a 'group' photo that was sent to him a month later. The group included women.

14

A New Life?

Jason and I moved into the new place. There was plenty of time for site seeing. That was all we could do is walk around the town. The movers would not be in our area for 4 more days, so we sat in an empty house with no comforts. There was no way to cook meals and we had run out of money. Yet, we started to laugh again. There was an illusion of peace that covered us for a couple days that could not make being without any type of human comforts steal our relief.

This was our homecoming and like battle weary soldiers we relished in the moment of victory. We were home. We were back in the West.

I had no idea that it was about to get worse. I had no idea that my life was going to be thrown into a battle to keep my sanity and question my safety.

I thanked God for that small reprieve; that moment when I believed that things were going to get better. I was happy for that moment, even if it was…..just for one moment.

I tried phoning Mack just before his two weeks were over in Chicago. Again, big mistake. I asked him why he just could not spare some time to phone me especially on the weekend that he wasn't "working" while he was in Chicago. This earned me a half hour worth of a lecture. He screamed at me that he didn't have the money to phone me from the States. If he used the hotel phone or his cell phone that would cost him $1,000. Money we don't have he yelled. To which my response was to let him know that every time I had gone to the States I just bought phone cards. Using the hotel phone with the cards gave me plenty of time to call people to let them know how my vacations were going and it only cost me $20 to make several calls. He wouldn't listen because he found an excuse that was a good one in his mind. Even though it was not reality based it was one he was going with and he even told me that he was not near any place to buy calling cards. Both lies.

If you can go downtown to eat out or go to entertainment events than you can stop somewhere to get a calling card. Any garage will generally sell them. Plus, a couple months later when I seen his cell bill, the charges for phoning me didn't even come to $20. The truth was that he just was having too much fun and did not want to call me.

Why do I try to get him to love me? When will I just finally raise my hands in the air and give up?

Mack came home from Chicago and dove into his new job. He left again almost immediately for Seattle. I had unpacked the boxed and organized the house while he was away. When he returned he told me that he had to go to Denver for a week. In between that time he had a conference that lasted as long, which included having dinner watching the horse races. (I don't know what else because once again I was only told that he 'never had fun at his job and it was boring' so according to him, he never had anything to say to me about it.)The new employer spared no expense on entertaining their new employees. I would see him in the evenings and he would let me know that he was tired and needed to rest from his hard day of work.

It was Montréal all over again.

My life consisted of sitting in a house with no means of going out or doing anything. I needed to stop expecting Mack to want to be a part of my life. He had his life and continued to show me that he did not need me in it.

My head and emotions started to circle each other knowing that the fight had started; I felt helpless and didn't know if I should support my head or my heart. I struggled in my confusion fighting for my sanity and then fighting for a marriage and relationship that I had stood before God and promised 'for better or worse, in sickness and in health'. I didn't know that it was only my husband's health and peace of mind that would matter in our relationship. Yet here I was once again on a roller coaster that I wanted to get off!

He came home one night and told me that he had to go on another two week trip again soon, then without 'talking' to me about it, went into the living room to watch a movie.

I followed him and sat in a chair facing him. I stared at him making it known that I wanted to talk, that I had something to say to him. I knew it was not going to be pleasant, so I thought I would wait for his permission to tell me I could speak to him.

"What the fuck do you want now?" he paused the movie and looked at me with hate and extreme annoyance in his eyes.

"I want my own vehicle." I said it without blinking or showing any form of cowardice in front of his blatant dislike of me. "It will allow me to get a job."

For a second I thought he was going to rant on about how we could not afford to get another one. But I saw his eyes fade their focus on me. He was thinking about something.

Finally, Mack looked back at me and stated "Fine, I will ask my dad to help us get you a truck."

A truck? I don't like trucks. ……..but, he just agreed to me having a vehicle. I waited; still watching him, not really knowing if the conversation held more to it or if I would be 'dismissed' from his presence so he could finish his movie.

He continued, "I want to buy a camper to go fishing so we will need a truck to haul it."

He said that just as I was starting to think of a way to ask for a car instead, I noticed his expression and then the familiar orders came harshly from his mouth; "You finished? Anything else, I want to watch my movie, so shut the fuck up if you want to stay in here."

I heard the back door closing. Jason must have gone out for a walk. He hated hearing the way his dad talked to me ....it was the same way Mack's dad spoke to and treated his wife. Mack and his dad seem to feel they had/have the right to humiliate or degrade their wife, a wife has no value; no worth other than keeping the house clean and not questioning what or why they do things.

I left him to watch his movie, walked upstairs to our bedroom, grabbed my bible and started searching for words of friendship and comfort. I needed Jesus to hold me while I cried in his lap and poured out my loneliness. Then I asked my LORD to have one of HIS angels blow up Mack's surround sound speakers. That way I wouldn't have to listen to the movie downstairs as if it was playing right next to the bed. Jesus did not do that for me and I quietly asked HIM to forgive my bitterness. I asked HIM to help me learn how to love Mack again. I drifted off into a restless sleep.

I woke up to Mack dreaming. I hated his dreams. I know that he had dreams of all sorts of things just like anyone else, but I hated the ones that told me it was about another woman. I hated them, because I felt that I was never 'the other woman'. I was about to leave the bed as I usually did and finish my night on the couch, when I stopped myself.

What if I did the opposite to what I usually do? What if I tried to include myself harder in Mack's life? Isn't he my husband? Didn't I want to have him show me affection? If he was in a mood for affection then shouldn't I as his wife be able to share that with him?

I reached over and placed my hand on him and started to kiss his cheek. I moved my body closer and imagined that he would like reality more than a dream.

"WHAT THE FUCK!" I was shoved almost out of the bed and heard him swear at me in french.

I quickly grabbed my pillow and went downstairs to finish the night alone and prayed that the rejection would end. I woke him up, it was my fault. I know how much he hates to be woken up at night. It was my fault.

The next morning I was engulfed in rage. Mack without saying a word to me all morning was now in his 'office' talking on the phone with someone that he obviously enjoyed talking to. When I had gone upstairs to our room to get dressed I stared at the bed sheets.

There was no knife that would have cut deeper. The knowledge that he got more fulfillment from his dream, his imagination and whoever it was that was in that dream, than he wanted to have from me; sliced me in two. I ripped the sheets from the bed, ran downstairs to put them in the washing machine but stopped in front of his office door first.

"You don't love me!" I screamed at him. "WHY DID YOU WANT TO MOVE WITH ME?!" I felt manipulated and used, yet I didn't know why or what for? "WHY do you want to be with a woman you are not attracted to????"

He looked at me calmly as if he had all the patients and time in the world to watch a lunatic rant.

"I don't know what you are talking about? Are you finished? I have to work." He was about to turn back to his desk and ignore me.

"This!" I showed him the bed sheets. "You would rather have sex in a dream than with me?!"

He looked at the sheets and after a silence of about three seconds got up, grabbed his computer bag and computer, cell phone and wallet then pushed past me to leave the house.

"You fucking crazy slut……….!" he swore continually at me , calling me disgusting things as he slammed his way out of the house, jumped into his car and squealed the tires as he left the driveway.

I sat on the floor crying for a long time before I picked myself up to do the task I had set my mind on; washing the sheets.

God help me! Why do I want my husband to show me that I please him physically? Why do I crave for my husband to make me feel like he would enjoy sleeping with me, rather than make me feel like I am now only good for 'relief' and then only when he was desperate ,been drinking or had been aroused by someone else.

I was not an ugly woman. …..but…..neither was I 18. I had some stretch marks on my stomach and wore the age of 39 years. Although I consistently got people expressing their amazed disbelief when they found out how old I was, it didn't help me now. Often when people seen my son and I together they thought that I was his girlfriend and not his mother.

Some strangers came up to me in a Chinese restaurant one time that I had taken Jason out for dinner, when he was 17 and incredulously asked if they had heard the young man correctly. 'Did he just call me 'mom'? Did they hear right? 'Did the young man just say "mom" to me?'

Jason and I laughed, I thanked them for their honoring compliment and assured them that 'yes' they heard him correctly and that 'yes' I was his mother.

I was also not a stranger to men making advances towards me.

I was not an ugly woman. Yet now, I felt repulsive, unattractive and unwanted. Not to mention an unwelcoming sensation of constantly being told that "I am not seeing what my eyes are seeing." One of the comments he threw at me before he left the house raging was that there was 'nothing' on the sheets I had just shown him. Even though I could see it and feel it….to Mack if he said he didn't do it or it wasn't true……then it just was as Mack said even if it opposed what you were seeing, feeling or hearing.

It was never as I seen things, it was always what he said was reality. Anything else equated insanity to him.

After we got married I wanted him to reassure me that the bed we were going to be sleeping in was new. He yelled, screamed and threw things around in anger to my questioning whether he was telling me the truth about the bed. I later found out that the bed 'was' new…..to him and his ex girlfriend, which made it, correct to say to me….'yes, the bed was new.' In his mind, misleading me or telling me a half truth was not telling me a lie. Or that is what he wanted me to believe. I knew that he was fully aware that his answer was a lie and meant to mislead my thinking; he just didn't want to be accused of lying. And, in his manipulating mode of 'playing with/on words; he knew exactly what he was doing and saying.

Again one evening we went downstairs to have dinner with his parent and I pleadingly asked him if it was alright with him that there was no drinking that night. He said, 'okay, no drinking'.

Later that evening he disappeared downstairs for awhile to get himself another can of coke. As the minutes passed I felt that he went downstairs to the bar that held all the strong liquor.

'He promised me!' I thought, and got up from the table to see if he was keeping that promise. He heard me coming down the stairs and I heard him moving things around fast. Then he met me at the bottom of the stairs smiling at me.

"We weren't going to drink tonight Mack." I stated.

"I never had a drink." He replied without hesitating and looking me straight in the eyes.

He started to open his can of coke to take a drink from it. 'Don't lie to me,' I thought and reaching up for his face I gave him a kiss on the lips.

"You taste like rum." And his breath was laced with the heavy sent of hard liquor.

"I never had a 'drink'," he scolded me harshly. "A DRINK, is in a cup. I never had a DRINK of alcohol!"

I didn't understand. If he didn't agree with the 'no drinking' tonight agreement that we made before dinner, then why did he not just tell me so. He could have said the truth. 'No Tammy, I like having a couple drinks with my meal and don't see anything wrong with it. Why did he have to lie twice to me that night, and add to the problem by giving him another reason to put me down and show his parents what a horrible wife I was. He was angry with me for the rest of the night calling me a watch dog and bitch.

Or, when he came home telling me that he was only with a bunch of men, and smelling like perfume. When I found out otherwise he told me in anger......"I wasn't WITH other women, they were WITH us".

His reality; he did not have 'a drink', it was a 'new' bed, he 'never' is 'with' other women.

Why did he want to get married? Why did he want to marry me? If he doesn't want to share a life with someone then why doesn't he just release me from this marriage contract and live his life in a manner that he desires. A manner in which he doesn't have to talk to someone, share with someone or even have someone around until he wants that someone around. Wouldn't he be happier to hire a house maid and live a single life? Keeping company with any woman he wants and not having to be responsible or faithful to any?

162

I finished the laundry and remade the bed. He never came home until 6:30, by which time I desperately wanted to have a glass of wine. I never used to be a drinker. There was a time I drank when I was at the legal age to get into a night club. I spent about two years of my life wasting it on partying, and when I look back I do believe that I wasted money and time in those years on nightclubs. Now though, I wanted to go to sleep without hoping for my husbands' arms to surround me. I didn't want to imagine that he was hoping to talk with me now that his day was done. I no longer wanted to think.

I sat at the table in silence. Mack put on a movie to watch in the living room. I pushed myself away from the table, grabbed my coat and called out to him that I was going to get a bottle of wine. I told him I would be back in 20 minutes. That is how long it would take for me to walk to the liquor store, buy some cheap wine and walk back. He didn't say anything to me, and I knew that I could not leave the house without telling him where I was going and how long I would be. There would be heck to pay if he had to ask me where I was or why I took so long in doing it. I learned that I had to tell him. He did not have to tell me.

A week later I had a used white truck in my name. Two more weeks after that we had a used camper trailer that needed a lot of things fixed in it.

Mack informed me that his mother was coming down for a visit and he wanted to take her camping. We worked on the camper at a break neck speed. We fixed the roof and the ceiling. We replaced the insulation, ventilation windows, light fixtures and paint on the ceiling all in one week. We changed the locks and handles on the door, ripped out the wallpaper and replaced it with vinyl. We took out old shelves, dirty curtains and stinking cushions. In just over two weeks the camper looked and smelled new when you walked in. Mack also replaced the old furnace with a new one, the whole time of fixing that camper we fought. It was all because of me, I was standing in the wrong spot, couldn't get him a tool fast enough, went ahead of him to do something he did not specifically tell me to do...etc.

Before we got the camper, Mack took me fishing with our tent to a lake almost 4 hours from our house to check and see if we would like it and if the fishing was good. I liked it there and was thankful that we had an older gentleman that was camping alone and tenting beside us to keep us company. He filled us with opportunity to have interesting conversation. If he hadn't been there things would not have gone smooth. I also learned that if Mack and I go camping, I am not to pack the car or unpack the car. I don't know what to take out or how to put it back. Instead of fighting and trying to insist that I was capable to initiate on my own what needs to be done to set up a tent or camp area, I just leave it to him. I learned that my job was to stick close to him so that I was available to go, get and do anything he told me to without having him have to call or tell me twice. I learned that I needed to put, place and do what he told me to the 'exact way' he wanted it, or I would only be asking for him to get upset with me.

The camper was finished, we knew where we were going to take her camping and she would be coming down in a week. This was not something I looked forward to.

The nice thing at this time was that Jason and I had both gotten jobs. I looked forward to going to work. The women that were my new co-workers were wonderful to me. This allowed me to not think about Mack's mother soon coming to visit.

I was not looking forward to being with one of the people that had so much control over my husband, enough so to change completely his personality into a whining, thumb sucking, 'I need my mommy', little boy. It didn't help that he would tell me that his mother was the only woman that deserved respect. He said that I was a slut, all women were sluts, that is except his mom. He would make it quite clear to me.....'GET IT IN YOUR HEAD' clear to me; that his mother was the only woman that deserved respect. Even though I heard him give 'respect' to any one of the secretaries that would phone him. They apparently deserved respect too. This was his circular way of talking to me. He would out and out yell at me that I was a slut. Then when I would respond by saying, 'you think I am a slut?' he would tell me that 'he never said that!' he said 'every woman was, except his mom.' I think this was his word game he always played on me to let me think that I could not accuse him of actually calling me a slut.

"Why do you think I am a slut?" I would argue with him whenever he yelled that name at me.

"I never said you were a slut!" he would scream back throwing or breaking things to make his point. "I said ALL women were sluts....." he would pause here," except my mother!"

"Mack you are telling me that I am a slut in that statement!" there were no tears now when he called me names. I was getting used to it. My hope in him liking me or thinking well of me was starting to completely die.

"I am not saying that you bitch!" he would yell at me with a red face. "Don't put words in my mouth, you fuck!"

I didn't think I ever put them in his mouth, but I was going to repeat the ones that came out.

15

Camping

"Where is the broom?" she asked me in a heavy French accent. We were almost finished packing the camper with the things we needed for the fishing trip.

"In the closet by the door as you enter the camper." I replied. His mother apparently wanted to sweep out the camper before we locked it.

I took a moment to watch her go back into the camper, I also watched as Mack was backing up the truck to hook the camper up to it.

I really had nothing against her except for resentment over the fact that Mack had shoved it in my face so much on how much he loved her more than me. I hated the fact that she fed that so much. She would always be running up to give Mack food that he liked to eat when I lived above her in Montréal. She would iron shirts for him and well; just 'take care of her son' because apparently I was not doing a good enough job. Any time he would mope around her, hanging his head down and looking like a lost puppy over the fact that he had married such a horrible person; she would give him sympathy as if he was a 5 year old little boy. I resented that at the age of 40, she would still not let her son be a man. She wasn't a mother to sit her son down and tell him to grow up and take responsibility for his new family, or encourage him to go to his wife for support rather than run to her. Both of them showed me that I was not needed to support, encourage or edify my husband; he would run to mommy and she would fill that role for him. Apparently it was not my job. So after two years of being shown by both of them that he was satisfied with her doing the job and she in turn was happy to do it, I gave it up.

I loved my son, yet in all the years in raising him I had impressed on him the fact that he needed to be responsible for his own actions and decisions he made in life. I wanted a relationship with Jason but I would not run after him and eat things out of his dinner plate just because he didn't want it there as she had done with Mack. I resented that even now mommy came first.

My biggest fault I felt as a mother was that I worried too much. This did not stop me from letting my son have his own life, but when he spent a night with a friend or was away from home for any reason; I always seemed to worry a little until he was home safe.

We were all in the truck ready to start our camping trip. 'My' truck meant 'I' drove. I inhaled the freedom of that knowledge, even though my nerves were raw with irritation as no sooner did I start pulling out of the driveway than mom and son started talking.

It took us almost 4 hours to get to the lake and then another hour to unhook the truck and set up the camper and then the inflatable dingy. A trip that you normally would hear Mack only say a couple sentences to me in was filled with nonstop conversation and laughter with his mother.

We cooked some lunch (or I should say Mack and his mother cooked lunch), ate and went fishing for walleye to have for supper.

Before we went out fishing I told Mack that it was the first day of 'that time of the month' for me and that I would go with them in the boat if he could get me back in time to 'change' my pad. He promised he would so we all got into the dingy and set out fishing.

I loved fishing and when I knew the right lure or technique to use would catch fish easily. That evening was no different. Mack caught some but his mother only caught one. This (I thought) was completely normal for a fishing trip. I remember going fishing with a good friend of mine that could have had his own angling show (because of how good he was at it), would always catch more than me. That was the story of fishing.

After almost two hours out on the lake, I could feel that I needed to get back to shore. I asked Mack if he would take me back so I could quickly change my pad.

"I want mom to catch another fish." He dismissed my request, "can't you wait?" then sounded annoyed that I wanted to interrupt his quest.

"No, Mack; I need to go back to the camper." I could feel that it already may be too late. I also took into account that it was going to take us almost another 30 minutes to motor back to our dock area. "I need to go back now." I stated.

He ignored my request with his actions. He kept fishing. Yet with his mouth he complied. "Yes okay, we will go back." Both he and his mother kept fishing.

An hour went by with them talking and fishing. I sat quietly holding my rod. My line was out of the water, and I waited for him to start for the shore. We motored in between other boats while he tried to find a better spot for his mother to catch fish.

I sat, unmoving as I felt the blood overflow my pad and spread out soaking into my jeans. I sat quietly as I knew the mess I was now sitting in would not be hidden when I got up. There was nothing I could do. It didn't matter to anyone in the boat. The promise was broken to get me back in time and I knew that I would have to get up and walk through the camp, back to the camper with a bloody mess in my jeans.

We finally went back to the dock two hours later. I didn't even look interested in cleaning the blood from the seat of the dingy where I had been sitting. I didn't show emotion. I got up out of the boat, looked at Mack and said, "I have to go clean myself up". I walked away as if nothing was wrong. I walked to the camper not caring who seen me or what they thought. I had no choice. What would that have done if I went angry or crying? It would have changed nothing.

As I changed my clothes, cleaned myself up and tried to wash out my underwear and jeans, Mack and his mother cleaned the fish and enjoyed each other's company by the lake side. I sat alone again when they returned with the fillets to prepare the meal in the camper.

I was called in when dinner was ready.

After dinner was over and everything was cleaned up, we started a card game.

I hated it. Mack through his derogatory comments every time I started to get ahead of his mother in points would add to my resentment of her. The camping trip was for her. He stated quite clearly that "I want my mom to have a good time," and "I want to make my mom happy". So, I started 'loosing' the game and wishing that it would end fast.

It finally did and we went to bed, they went to sleep and I stayed awake crying inside with self pity and full of building anger.

His mother. She could do and say anything to him. I on the other had to watch what I say to Mack even more than I ever had. Now he was starting to physically shove me around. He would add shoving me out of his way along with his 'f off, or get the f away from me, or just because I was standing in a place he wanted to be. For example, if we were in the kitchen and he wanted to get into a drawer or cupboard where I happen to be standing; he would either use his hands to shove me out of the way or just whip open the door/drawer allowing it to hit me and force me out of his way.

A couple days ago in my stupidity, I once again asked him 'why he couldn't talk to me the way he just talked on the phone to a lady he worked with'? He answered by grabbing me by the throat and pushing me up against the bathroom wall. While his hands were pushing on and around my throat he held me there until he had finished screaming and yelling two inches from my face a string of curses and vile names. He finished by throwing me away from him and saying, "It is all in your head you insane slut; I treat all sluts the same"!

I knew the soft laughter I heard and gentle tone in his voice while he was on the phone with her was not in my head. I also knew that when he was speaking with a male co-worker, his voice was more 'matter of fact' and a little louder in volume. It wasn't as soft and low like when a woman would phone him.

The next morning of our fishing/camping trip, it started all over. The trip was all about mommy. I didn't even know why I was asked to come along. This time though, when we went out fishing after breakfast I put on three pads two of which were placed side by side. I walked like I had a huge diaper on. No one cared anyway.

We were in the boat for about two hours again and I was catching fish one after another. I was talking to the water, talking to the fish. "Come on you know you want the hook," I would say looking down into the gently rolling water. I held a one sided, comical conversation with the fish. Mack and his mother held their own conversation.

All of a sudden Mack showed annoyance bordering on anger towards me as I pulled in another fish to the boat.

"Would you stop that!" he stated with exasperation.

I stared at him in disbelief. "What?" I asked. We are fishing. Did he want me to stop catching fish?

"Why don't you give your fishing rod to mom, I think she can't feel when a fish bites with the rod she has," he commanded.

I stared at him for a second trying to quickly asses how serious he was with his request. It didn't take too long to show me how serious he was when he went to reach for my rod.

"Okay." I allowed him to change our rods over.

Two minutes after I dropped my line in the water, I caught another fish. Now he didn't hide his annoyance with me.

"Change seats with my mom." He commanded not so gently.

Resentment burst into my heart pushing its way through my veins. 'You could not be happy for me that I am having a good day fishing?' I thought angrily. He couldn't be happy with me and just in conversation make a request like, 'Hey Tammy, you must have a lucky spot. Do you think mom could catch some fish in that spot?'

No, he had to show me that he was not impressed that I was catching fish and his mother wasn't.

I understood that he desired for his mother to enjoy this fishing trip and that included actually to catch a fish. Yet why would it be at my expense? Why did that have to include hurting me?

I got up and changed seats with her. Then I only dropped my line into the water just letting the hook dangle a couple inches under the surface of the water. I didn't want to get him madder if I caught another fish. I sat there like a dummy holding my rod knowing for me the fishing trip was over.

We were out for just over four hours before we were back at the dock. Mom and son went to the fish cleaning tables by the docks to fillet the fish. I walked back to the camper alone.

I didn't go back fishing with them that day. I ate with them but sat at the camper for the rest of the day.

Alone. Yes, sulking inwardly and licking my proverbial wounds.

It was the straw that broke the camel's back.

There was nothing I could do to make him love me. There was nothing I could do to make him talk or treat me like he did his family, friends or co-workers. There was nothing I could do to make him care.

That evening I snapped.

"You don't want to be with me!" I cried out to Mack after supper. "Why did you bring me camping if everything to you is about giving your mom a wonderful camping trip?" I was spurred on by the fact that I was completely bored and had drank two glasses of wine and had one beer in me. I wasn't drunk because I started drinking at noon, had two meals and 7 hours to drink them within. Yet that was enough to give me a little courage. I was tired of being nothing to him. I wanted to leave them to have their happy time without me.

Mack and his mother both looked at me like I was a stupid, unreasonable person. Maybe I was unreasonable at that time but I was not stupid.

I jumped into the truck and told them that I was going to stay in it until they needed me to drive them back home. I drove the truck down to the docks, parked and sat staring at the water.

Neither one of them cared that I had left. My husband didn't care at all. There was no reassurance from him that he didn't mean to make me feel unwanted or anything to indicate that he cared I was going to stay in a truck for a couple days while they finish their camping and fishing trip. He didn't even watch me drive away in the truck before he turned his back on me and continued to sit at the fire with his mother that evening. They continued talking.

In the truck, staring out the window into the night, I started to cry. I think I cried for a couple hours straight. I prayed to God and asked HIM why I married a man that did not love me? Why didn't HE stop me? But, not knowing what I knew now about Mack, would I have listened to God if HE had tried to stop me. And; maybe God did try to stop me in the voice of two of my friends that didn't think a leopard could change his spots no matter how old he was.

I thought about all the times that Mack showed me that he just did not care.

We had gone to a car wash in Montréal to have his car washed. I got out and told him that I was going to get a cup of coffee next door to have with a cigarette. I went; bought a small coffee because that was all the money I had and went outside to drink it and smoke one cigarette. When I was finished my cigarette, I walked back to the car wash which was only a couple feet away from the coffee shop.

He was gone. The men were surprised to see me knowing that I had come with Mack. 'He paid and then left', they told me. I asked them again speaking in french and they looked at the back of the shop to see if he was in the alley waiting for me. He wasn't. He left me there.

I had no money for a bus and I had no one to call to pick me up. I started walking back to the apartment. It was almost noon and I thought I could make it home before supper if I just walked straight there without stopping.

I carried the little coffee I had left in the cup saving it for when I would want another cigarette in about an hour. Rain clouds started to gather above and I prayed that it would not start raining until I got home. I was only in a little pair of shorts, light shirt and flip flops.

I had a couple cat calls and whistles as cars drove by me on the boulevard, I ignored them all. After walking for some time there was a honk and I could feel that a vehicle had slowed down to get my attention. 'Was it

Mack?' I thought. I looked up to see a van and an older man waving to me. Again I ignored this, maybe he thought I was someone he knew. I kept walking.

The van must have turned around because pretty soon I seen it again pulling into a parking lot beside me. The man called out to get my attention.

"Hey, can I talk to you?" he asked.

I stopped and made sure that I was far enough away from him and his van, if he wanted to grab me, he would have to make a run for it and the distance gave me a head start to get away.

"What?" I responded.

"I noticed that you are walking alone and you look lonely carrying that cup of coffee so I thought you would like to talk." He smiled at me and it made me sick.

"No thank you, I don't need to talk to anyone." I was about to turn and continue my walk when he quickly spoke again to me.

"I want someone to talk to and you look like someone I could trust." He added, "I am lonely and just need someone to talk to, I am not interested in having sex or anything; I just want to talk to you."

'Do I look like a five year old that could be enticed by some candy to get into the van with you?' I thought and in disgust I turned away from him.

"No," I threw loudly over my shoulder as I walked away making sure he wasn't jumping out of his van to come after me. "I don't want to talk."

I continued to walk down the sidewalk this time with a little quicker pace.

'God thank you for protecting me.' I prayed. 'Thank you for never leaving me or forsaking me.'

Within an estimated 10 minutes from that encounter, I felt another vehicle slow behind me and I knew it was going to stop beside me right there on the road.

I never ran, but stiffened myself for a fight as I turned to see who it was.

It was Mack. If I hadn't had an encounter that took my feeling of safety away, I would have ignored him and kept walking. Instead, I got into the car and while buckling the safety belt asked him, "Why did you leave me?"

"You left me!" he spat out and drove home weaving angrily in and out of traffic.

That was the excuse he gave himself for leaving me when he knew that I was only going to get a small coffee. Again, it was my fault. But, I was thankful that he showed up so quickly after that other man had tried to pick me up.

Then a flash of thought crossed my mind. I remembered when I had gone to the corner store for a coffee and was told by the owner that Mack was in his car watching me through the window. Was Mack following me too? Is that why he picked me up so quickly after that other guy tried too because he didn't want someone else picking me up?

No, that wasn't possible.

He left me another time when we went down to go clean his boat. The boat was docked on Lake Champlain in New York State.

It was a warm day and he had pulled his folded up dingy from the trunk of his car and began putting it together on the dock. I had no experience as to how to put one together at that time and unfortunately had to wait for him to tell me what to do.

He cursed at me and made sure I noted with all his body language of hitting the dingy and swearing at it was really to assure me that he was mad at me, not the dingy.

A man he knew came along and asked if he could help him with his dingy.

Mack took the aid of this man and I stepped back and out of the way so they could put it together without my interference.

After the dingy was in the water and tied to the dock, we both got into his car to go meet with another of his friends. The two of them were going to move the sailboat from the dock it was at to the one that the dingy was now at.

As soon as Mack started to pull out of the driveway he immediately started screaming at me, calling me names, driving angrily, smashing and punching the interior of the car and ripping me emotionally apart.

His rage was not going to stop; I couldn't see why he would be so mad just because I couldn't help him put his dingy together. I had tried. I had to get away from him. He was too mad and I didn't know why. I tried to ask what I did wrong to which he ignored me and continued his verbal attack. I then started to yell at him to stop the car.

This seemed to make him madder but I had to get away from him. There was no reason that he should be this angry and no reason to be mad at me. I never said anything to him about anything other than asking him what he wanted me to do. Did the man that had helped him remind him of sailing with his ex girlfriend? Was he a friend of Mack's that was no longer considering Mack a friend because of his break up with his ex? Whatever triggered him, I could not take his rage.

He jerked the car across the opposite lane almost causing an accident with an oncoming car, and screeched to a halt in the parking lot of a green house store.

I jumped out and ran to some grass and sat down allowing some tears to fall quietly while cradling my emotional pain. I didn't know what to do. I sat for a few minutes and desperately wanted to have a smoke. Mack was sitting in his car. The parking lot was empty except for him. He still looked like he was full of rage and I knew that I didn't want to go back to the car right now. I had to calm down and let him calm down too. Then I noticed the green house was next to a drug store.

'They would have cigarettes,' I thought. I got up and started to walk to the drug store and noticed that Mack started the car.

When I came out of the drug store, he was gone. I looked around to see if he had parked somewhere else. He hadn't. I went back to the grass where I had been sitting and sat once again.

I had very little money, maybe $20. My cell phone did not work in the States and even if it did, I had no one to call. I kept checking my cell phone to see if he was going to call me from his. Nothing; there were no texts or missed calls. No attempt by him what-so-ever to find out if I was ok, or even where I was at this point. I had no way of getting back to Canada or the apartment. I sat there for a couple of hours.

'Father,' I prayed; 'if I can make it home this time, then can I promise myself to never be put in this position again?' I asked to feel the presence of Jesus. I didn't want to be alone. I believe, in His mercy He showed me that I was not alone, that with God; I was never alone. I felt drawn into the green house store. As I walked through the doors, I noticed an older woman working by the till. The place was empty of people, just her and I.

I went up to her and before talking, I felt compassion for me flowing from her. I knew at that moment that Jesus had gone before me to take care of the situation once I asked Him to take it.

"I only have a Canadian 20 dollar bill," I started; "Could I give it to you to pay for a quick, one minute phone call?"

Then she did a surprising thing. She came up to me and gave me a hug. I immediately started to cry again.

"You are going to be Okay," she told me softly. "Keep your money, and I will dial your call for you."

I told her Mack's cell number which for her would be long distance. She dialed it on the stores phone, and then gave the phone to me.

He answered. He was with his friend that apparently didn't care where I was either.

"Well?" I asked him unsure of what to even ask him.

"Well what?" he responded.

"You are in control Mack." I patted him on the back for showing that he was all powerful and that he could do, say and act anyway he wanted to. "I have no money to get home. Can you phone the greyhound and buy a ticket for me?"

"If that is what you want." He stated with no emotion.

'IF THAT IS WHAT I WANT!' I wanted to cry out to him and shake him into having any type of human feelings for another person but himself.

Instead, I repeated myself. "You are in control Mack you decide if you want to pick me up where you dropped me off to go sailing with you, or; you don't want me with you and you buy a bus ticket for me to go home."

"I'll come and get you." He stated flatly and hung the phone up. I knew as I hung up the phone that he did not want to pay for a bus ticket more than he actually wanted me to be with him.

I thanked the lady and told her, "I pray God will bless you and give you as much mercy as you have shown me......a complete stranger to you today."

As I waited for Mack outside on the same grassy spot, I vowed that I would never again be dropped off somewhere and then left by him. I would never leave on a trip with him without enough money on me to take care of myself if he ever abandoned me again.

He picked me up 40 minutes after the call. We went sailing as if nothing ever happened. The only explanation he ever gave to me for being so hateful and hurtful to me that day was ...."You must have said something to piss me off."

So, it was my fault. I deserved it.

I sat behind the steering wheel of the truck remembering how often he had even left me at home.

He would just get into his car and leave telling me that I made him so miserable that he was going to go kill himself. He would then come home whenever he wanted to and didn't care if he worried me. He never had to tell me where he was going. He didn't have to. He just simply put, did not care. And the only explanation he ever gave me to why he did this was......

......."You must have said something."
......."You must have done something."
...... "You must have pissed me off."

He never did or said anything wrong. Ever.......but....'IF' he did do or say something wrong.......it was never his fault because...........

"I must have pissed him off."

He never had to say sorry and mean it. He never had to be sorry or care. He had only himself to answer to and he felt he agreed with himself and was always right in his words and actions. But he could admit that "IF" he ever did do something that was not quite right............well, it was someone else's fault.

I stopped crying and looked at the time. It was after midnight and the truck was cold. My eyes hurt from crying. My chest hurt from emotional pain.

I knew that Mack and his mother were comfortably sleeping in the camper without me.

I knew this was not what I was supposed to think, but...... what if I were to leave him? They obviously did not care if I was here or not. So, why can't I leave and do to him like he has shown me that he could do to me at any time he wanted to.

The only difference was that he and his mom have money. They will have to phone AMA (which he has a membership with) to tow the camper home after their vacation together or phone me to pick them up.

I don't have to sit in a truck for a couple days. I could go home. So, I started the truck engine and headed back to the camper to get my stuff and leave them all the fishing gear that was in the back of the truck.

16

Separation

I pulled the truck up in front of the camper, jumped out and went immediately to the box of it and climbed in to pull out all the fishing rods and tackle box. I put these against the picnic table and went back for the net and cooler bag. I continued this until the box of the truck was empty. Then I went to the camper door to go in and get my things out of it.

I turned the door knob and found it to be locked.

'He could not hurt me anymore,' I lied to myself. Inside of myself I was completely broken. I had been correct in surmising that they had finished their evening and had gone to bed in peace. The locked door told me that they were not interested in having me back and content with the thought of finishing their little holiday without me.

I banged on the camper door knowing that I was doing the forbidden sin. I was going to wake him up.

I heard him swearing inside the camper as he got up to unlock the door.

He came out as I tried to push my way past him to go inside and get my purse, cell and packed bag.

"You fucking bitch! What the fuck do you want! I thought you said you were going to sleep in the truck?" he spat out with words dripping in hate.

"I changed my mind! I am not going to stay up here and sleep in a truck while you and your mom continue to camp!!" I replied. I tried again to get past him to get my things.

By this time his mother, also angry with me came out of the camper yelling at me.

He grabbed my shirt in front of my throat with his fist and pushed it into my throat. "You fucking unreasonable slut! Go to sleep somewhere and leave us alone!" He said more things and his mother was mimicking him with her mouth standing right behind her son.

"I am going to!" I yelled back as he jerked me around. "I am going to go home and let the two of you finish your camping trip without me!"

The hateful, hurtful words started flying at me by not only him but also his mother. He would only pause long enough to let his mother be heard. Then he would continue. He threatened me and demanded that I give him the truck keys. 'He didn't care about me' but he was not going to let me take off with the truck and ruin his mothers camping trip! He shoved me around and yelled so close to my face that he was spitting in it. He knocked me towards the camper and for a second I saw that his mother appeared to want to do the same. He grabbed my clothes in front of my chest and pushed them up into my face almost lifting me off the ground with them as he pushed me into the side of the camper.

His fist and forearm pressed into my mouth as he ripped the keys out of my right hand. He held me there unleashing more names and curses into my face......into my soul. I felt pain along with a small snapping sound in my mouth and new that he had just broke my tooth. He pressed harder into my face and I tasted blood fill my mouth as the pressure was slowly tearing my lips open.

"You evil fucking monster!" he continued the verbal onslaught along with his mother and then.....I no longer cared.

I wanted him to stop.

I could not make him stop his treating me like he did. His parents and family members applauded it and encouraged it. His co-workers and friends all seen me as a bitch and pitied him for having to live with such an awful woman. This was my fault too. When he went out of town

184

with his co-workers to the States, I took that opportunity to scream at him, to express how much he was hurting me. It was an opportunity to let him know how much he hurt me, to let him know how I felt and because he was so far away he couldn't hurt me. I screamed at him that I wanted a divorce! He would rant on to his co-workers telling them that I was such a horrible person. They agreed with him. But when he came home he would act like he missed me and that he loved me so much. I would change my mind on getting a divorce. I would again hope that he meant it and that we could love and respect one another. It never lasted and the next time he left for a trip, he again didn't even pretend the slightest interested in phoning me. Not for our anniversaries, my birthdays or our son's. He just did not care to ever talk to me while he was out with his co-workers. No one was willing to tell him that he could not treat another human being like this. They all believed I deserved it, and I now believed I did too. I must be a hateful horrible person. So many people thought of me like that right now, so it must be true.

And then I thought of the police. The police in the West were different than Quebec police. Here they encourage respect and protection for every family member.

Once he let me go, I phoned the police using his cell phone. I don't think he thought that I was actually going to. Maybe because I had threatened before and never did. This time I was not going to stop the call. He was 'resting' by the campfire now with his mother as they patted each other on the back verbally for how well they handled the bitch. They were satisfied that now that they had the truck keys, I could do nothing else.

"I want you to tell my husband to stop calling me names and that he can't do this!" I pleaded with the person that answered the 911 call I made.

They asked me where I was and that they were going to send out a police cruiser immediately. They asked me if I could get somewhere safe and wait for them. I said yes and agreed/arranged to meet them at the camp registration office.

Safe? Why would I want to 'get somewhere safe'? What did it matter if he killed me now? What was left of my life worth saving? What was left of me? Was I not already dead inside?

I found it hard to talk and every swallow I tasted my own blood, but I still needed to talk. I called my son and asked him to pray for me. I knew that phone call to Jason had just broken any hope of him respecting his dad, probably for the rest of Jason's life. He was fuming mad and I heard anger in his tone I never heard before. He would never be able to respect a man that hurt his mother so much.

I also called my uncle and asked him the same thing. I was more than nothing of a human being at that point. My uncle was enraged when he heard Mack and his mother still spewing curses out at me in the back ground. Did Mack and his mother not think that I was really talking to someone? Did he think I was joking?

We have had our fights before but when he allowed his mother to join him in slamming me, this and this alone was what gave me the courage to actually call 911. My resentment of her. I took the abuse from him but I WOULD NOT TAKE IT FROM HER! He wanted someone on his side to hurt me, well then, I was going to beg for someone to stand with me. He had to stop it! The mental abuse had to stop! I cared less about the physical abuse than the mental abuse. The physical hurt less.

I just wanted him to love me. I wanted him to want the same thing as me. I wanted him and I to be each other's best friend. I wanted him to stop calling me names,

186

ignoring me when he wasn't mad at me and then putting me down when I wanted to know that he cared about me.

Why couldn't he share his life with me? Why couldn't he have talked to me and plan with me what we were going to do for his mother on this visit? He made the plans with her and her alone. He 'told' me what they decided they were going to do and I had to follow along like a dog. He 'planned' with others, he 'told' me.

I did it all wrong. I messed everything up! Anything I tried to do to get him to show me that he cared ended up proving to me how much he really didn't. This made me even more desperate to make him show me he cared. The circle went around, getting worse and producing more hate from him. Mack would love whom he wanted to and no one was going to make him change his mind.

I kept his cell phone and started walking to the office. He spoke to his mother and then I heard him following me.

He would not do anything else to me. I felt sure of this because I knew that the police were on their way. He was going to present himself as a wonderful person that had to deal with a rotten wife (or son as he had in Quebec). I sat on the steps of the dark office and waited.

Mack was soon beside me and sat down also on the steps. I tried not to look at him. I failed. I looked over to him and saw that his eyes were black with hate.

"Why are you such a monster?" he asked me calmly....coldly." he stared at me for a couple seconds and then we saw a spot light shining out a window of an oncoming car. It was a police car and it was driving slowly down the dirt road in our direction.

"You are bleeding Tammy." He brought his hand up towards my face as if he wanted to wipe the blood from my face.

I jerked my head away from him. I didn't believe he cared that I was bleeding. I felt he was more concerned that I needed to look like an out of control crazy woman, to uphold any story he was going to tell. I thought he was going to be believed again, why would anyone believe me? He didn't want me to look like a woman that needs protection. He wanted me to look like the woman he told everyone that I was. No one believed me. I felt lost and very alone.

A small voice inside of me told me that my son believed me, but that was because he suffered from his dad's character like I did; and no one believed him either. My uncle believed me. The thought flickered through my mind. Someone believed me! But my uncle had verbal proof as he heard Mack and his mother in the background of our short conversation.

A police woman came and shown her light on us and asked me to come to the car and told Mack not to go anywhere, he was just to stay right where he was.

Mack nodded his head patiently and stayed sitting on the office steps.

She asked me what happened.

I told her that I was sorry for phoning them, but....."I guess I am having a woman's self pity temper tantrum," I looked at her and tried not to cry, tried not to show how damaged and broken I was inside.

"I was going to sleep in the truck tonight, but I decided that I wanted to leave my mother in law and husband to finish their camping trip without me." I had nothing to hide. I was miserable and thought that if I needed to be taken away and locked up then I was not going to fight anything anymore. I just wanted the pain to stop.

I told her everything that happened that day, including that I had two glasses of wine and one beer starting at lunch time that day. It was now I believe 1 o'clock in the morning. I told her that I thought that I had enough determination in me to stay in a truck while my husband and his mother finished their camping trip but I broke. I couldn't do it. I wanted to leave, but my husband didn't want me to leave with the truck.

Another police car was there by that time and I retold the man everything. He was going to go and talk to Mack, but before he walked away I quickly told him.... "Please don't arrest him!" I was afraid all of a sudden that they would do more than just 'break up a domestic dispute'. "Please! Just tell him to stop calling me names!" I sounded pathetic and hated myself even more for sounding as stupid as Mack would pound into my head at times that I was. "Please," I tried again, "Just tell him that he can't do that anymore."

The male officer left to talk to Mack and I stayed with the woman officer still talking to her about the night.

Mack's mom was now with them. Then I saw Mack get up and turn around. The police officer reached for his handcuffs and placed them on Mack's wrists behind his back.

My body went cold.

They walked past us to get to the other police cruiser that was behind the one the woman officer drove.

As the male cop passed us, I asked in a panicked tone, "What are you doing?" Mack answered for him.

"This is what you wanted!" I could feel the hate from Mack as he walked past me even though he was never closer than 6 feet from me before he was placed in the back seat of the police cruiser. "This is exactly what you wanted Tammy!"

His mother called out to the male officer, "Where are you taking him?"

"He is going to spend the night in the jail maam." He stated calmly.

"Then I am going with him!" she asserted. "Wait for me!"

The male officer politely told her that she will not be able to go into the cell with him, but he could drop her off at a hotel in town. She ran back to the camper to get her bag. When she returned she pointed at me and told the police...."I never want to see her again."

'Don't worry.' I promised her in my heart silently, 'You never again will see me.'

Both police officers looked at me, I thought; almost in disbelief or maybe just an unspoken question on their face; 'is she joking? She wants to go to jail with her son?'

'No,' I answered back in my head. 'She can't let her 'baby' grow up and ever take responsibility of his own; she has to 'hold' him.'

Will she ever let him grow up? Wasn't I the one that was supposed to promise before God "till death do us part" when I married Mack, or was I grossly mistaken and should have taken a seat to let mommy come up and stand before the minister to say that line. Looking deep into her son's face, in front of all the witnesses present and say..'Till death do us part son.'

She made me sick.

Thiers was not a 'normal' mother – son relationship. She was his best friend, confidant, care taker, supporter and everything else a wife should be to a man, accept maybe without the sex.

That is why he lets other people fight his battles with/for him. And that is why he is too much of a coward to fight or stand up for someone else. She never let him grow up.

I wish I would have known that I was not just marrying Mack, I had married mommy as well.

A strange thought of Princess Diana flashed through my mind of when the world found out that on their 'honey moon', Prince Charles had brought his mistress along with them. Diana was not his true love. The mistress was.

"Tammy do you understand?"

I looked blankly for a second not sure that I would ever understand anything again. The officer was talking to me but I was answering with a numb mind. "That is not what I want Mack. This is not what I want."

I looked at the two officers and asked if they would mind if I had a cigarette.

No, neither minded and the woman produced a lighter and lit my cigarette for me.

I don't remember the rest of the conversation other than I believe they talked about taking pictures of me, particularly my face.

I hadn't looked in a mirror and didn't know what I looked like. I agreed absently to the pictures. The male officer left with Mack and his mother. I got into the police car with the woman and we drove to the camper.

She took pictures of me. Asked me to fill out some questions on a sheet of paper for her, and informed me that with evidence noted by officers of any domestic scene, an officer was to take responsibility to place someone under arrest even if it was against the victims' wishes. She said that, like me, a lot of women refuse to press charges.

I won't press charges, I told her. 'What for?' I thought to myself. This is my entire fault. Not his. I should have just sat in the shadows and let him enjoy his mommy.

I stayed in the camper for the rest of that night. I left the next morning without it. I needed someone to help me hook it up and get the boat.

Before the woman officer left last night she told me that the courts will probably put a peace bond on him to make sure he cannot come near me until he is acquitted or charged. She also asked if she could have victims' services contact me. I told her yes.

Now what?

The only one I wanted to be with right now was Jesus. I wanted to go home and just sit in his presence and cry. I wanted to feel him near me and needed to know that even if everyone else hated me that God was still okay with liking me. Even though I didn't deserve it. I was too wretched a human being.

17

Fighting Demons

I paced the house and sorted through cupboards. I cleaned the washroom and sanitized the floors. I dusted fake plants and washed windows. I went through my cloths and threw away everything that I had not worn in months. I wiped down the fridge, stove and counters. I weeded the garden and cleaned the garage. I scrubbed the stairs and cleaned out the boot and coat closet by the door. I washed the bedding including the duvet cover.

I ate nothing and hardly slept. I never went into any room of the house or outside without carrying the cordless phone. I tried to keep the phone line clear in case I got 'the call'.

Finally it came. I was in the kitchen cleaning out the fridge when the phone rang. It was the police.

Mack was going up before the judge a couple days after our horrible camping trip. If he pleaded guilty he would probably have to pay a fine and would be home that same night. If he wanted to fight it and plead innocent then we would be apart for possibly a year.

I answered the phone on its first ring.

"Could I speak with Tammy please?" I heard a now familiar voice on the other end of the phone. The arresting officer identified himself and continued to speak after I told him I was who he wanted to speak with.

"Tammy; your husband has had his case heard and he is pleading innocent."

I almost had to fight for words. "What?" I asked in confusion. 'How was he innocent?' 'And what is going to happen from here,' I thought to myself as he continued to talk.

"Tammy, your husband has stated that he was only trying to save your life."

I tried to listen between the lines. I tried to hear anything in his voice that would tell me more than his words were telling me. Yet to little avail, he was 100% professional and probably dealt with cases such as mine all the time.

"I don't understand." I responded in confusion. "How was he saving my life?"

"Your husband went before the judge and stated that you were extremely drunk and became uncontrollable." He paused for a second as though he was reading something. "He stated that when you told him you were going to drive home; he, being concerned for your safety didn't want you to drive drunk and possible kill yourself." There was another pause. "He stated that he needed to take the keys away from you so you would not harm yourself."

He was the hero husband that only had concern for his screwed up wife. He was a sales man. He knew how to present information with confidence; Mack knew how to get people to believe him.

I believed everything he said despite the fact that his actions didn't match his mouth when we were dating. I believed every time he would tell me that he loved and missed me every time he was away from me when he came home. Even though he never tried to phone, email or text me the whole time he was away from me, whether it was one day or two weeks. I believed him when he told me he loved me even after he had told me how much he hated me and called me so many vile names. Everyone believed Mack. He never did anything wrong, and if he did; it was someone else's fault.

"The trial is going to be in January Tammy and you will be called to testify for the Crown at that trial." He continued.

I sat at the table listening to the officer inform me that his mother had put a statement in to back up his story. I listened to him tell me that the judge ordered a peace bond against Mack to make sure he stays away from me until the trial. I heard him tell me that I was going to be brought up to the town named, given a room and meals that I did not have to pay for, and counsel. He spoke about the process to me. He gave me all the details and was going to have victims' services meet with me to help me through this process.

"I don't want to press charges." I said, hoping he would give me some hope as to getting out of fighting my husband in court.

"Tammy, the crown is pressing charges, not you." He continued to give me more details on what was going to happen and what was going to be expected of me.

We finished our conversation and I thanked him for his kindness in phoning me. He promised to keep me up to date with what was going on and gave me his direct line at the police station if I needed to contact him for any reason.

Once I hung up the phone, I cried. I cried and didn't even know from what angle the anguish was coming from. Was it for what my son had to go through? Was it for me? Was it for Mack?

I mourned for my son. He was so happy before I married Mack. He was smart and knew what he wanted in life. He trusted God. He always had a reason to smile and shared his humor willingly. His laughter had been contagious.

Now, he had earrings, tattoos, blue hair and the memory of living with such deep torment that he tried to hurt himself several times and kill himself twice.

One man did that to him and it was because of me. I married the man that hurt my son.

I vaguely remembered sitting across from one of my co-workers during one of our breaks at Tim Horton's, when was that, a lifetime ago? Mack had just proposed; I had accepted, and my son was extremely happy he would have his dad in his life; 'a dad' in his life for the first time.

"Tammy, there is a reason an ex is an ex." He told me while stirring some sugar into his coffee.

"Well, I believe people can change." I supplied back. "He is older and hopefully more mature."

"I remember my first girlfriend that I loved with all that I could love her with." He leaned on the table with his elbows while placing both hands around his cup and told his story of a first love and betrayal.

"I had received a couple letters from her after that but I knew that this is who she was and I no longer wanted her as a wife." He looked at me with respect for who I was and seemed to show concern for the decision I was about to make.

"You are making your decision based on the fact that you believe he changed." He waited a brief instant to see that I acknowledged this fact. Satisfied he continued..... "Remember who he was when you first dated him a long time ago. Remember 'why' you broke up with him when you did. Remember that he rejected the responsibility of raising his son or helping raise him in any way. You know that he has lived his life for only himself from that time, a long time ago until this time, today." He dropped his head a little and locked his eyes with mine; making it clear that he was going to say something else he did not want me to miss.

"Now Tammy, based on these reflections ....would you marry someone like that?"

That felt like a lifetime ago. I was a completely different person. Jason knew who he was then and I knew who I was.

Now, I could walk into a room; see a cupboard door open and panic. My mind would almost spin in a frenzy to solve this 'big' problem. 'If I closed it and he wanted it open, then I was going to get yelled at.' 'If I leave it open and he wanted it closed, I would get yelled at.' 'If I left it open and he forgot that he was the one that left it open in the first place, then I would get yelled at for forgetting to close cupboard doors.'

Before; I used to put almost 35000 kilometers per year on my car. I drove across Canada a couple times, into the United States and everyday because of my job or just life in general. I have been driving for 24 years. Now, I wasn't confident enough to drive in a big city.

Was I crying for myself? That I believed Mack when he said 'yes' to me that he was a Christian, because I made it completely clear that I could only marry a man that would go to church with me. Now, he tells me he was wrong, that he isn't and that I just need to 'suck it up'.

Was I crying because I believed in my vows and he didn't? For better or worse, in sickness and health.........till..........death do us part.

The sick, out of place thought slipped through my mind. Was it a death certificate I signed or a wedding certificate? I pushed it away and tried to believe in a happy ending.

Was I crying for him? He had a wonderful carefree life that fed his desires and had no real responsibilities other than to please himself. Now, he is being asked to have responsibility, and think of someone else besides himself. Now, he lives with someone that does not share his interest in serving one self but instead someone wanting to serve the Creator of the Universe and HIS son Jesus. It was a completely different world for him.

I didn't have to worry about Mack right now. He was with his mom and I knew she would be taking good care of him. Apparently from what I heard from others, Mack was doing fine. After the trial him and his mother left the small town where he had to stay to appear before the judge, came into the major City nearby and is site seeing and being tourists together. He was even taking her to a large mall that he would rather 'kill himself before he went with me to'.

I had to go back to work, and didn't know how to explain what happened to my mouth. My week off from work had turned into a nightmare. Or was it just a 'normal' part of my life now?

Maybe I should have just stayed in the truck until they finished camping. Or better yet maybe I should have just kissed mommy's _____, along with Mack. Maybe I should have just left that night without telling him.....but, no; I needed my purse from the camper. Maybe........

I cried all day and the rest of the night. I ate nothing and I slept almost not at all.

I phoned every Ministry team that I have ever tithed to and asked them to pray for my situation. I asked for them to pray that I would know what God wanted me to do, not what others were telling me to do. I phoned my long time friend that was my matron of honor at my wedding. I knew she loved the LORD with all her heart. I phoned my sister, my dad and my uncle. I asked everyone to pray for my situation. That I would do God's will and not mine. I wasn't looking for advice because I understood that my emotions were in control right now and I needed to be free from turmoil before making a serious choice.

The next day, I put on my uniform and went back to work.

Everyone knew. Everyone I worked with talked about it. I thought before too much gossip swam around the place I would talk to my employer myself and let her know what happened. Let her know what was happening in my life. I also needed her to know because I would need the time off to go to court and stand before a judge and fight against my husband. I didn't want to do that. I didn't want him to go to jail. I just wanted him to treat me like he does someone else that he cared for.

It was Montréal all over again. My personal home life was being reflected in my job.

Looking back on my life as a single mother and all the problems that arose from being in that position, I could not think of any problem I had to face that was bigger than this one. My life was not perfect and there were several scary or low points, but nothing that was this big or that was taking this long to deal with. And there was nothing I couldn't laugh through or about once it was over. Including one winter that I had received notice to have my heat turned off. After phoning the gas company and letting them know what I could afford to pay each month, I then immediately started planning with my son ways to keep warm in the house. We prayed about the unexpectedly large, end of the year gas bill and set about dealing with it like it was a challenge we could handle. I believe God answered our prayers. The gas was not shut off and they accepted the plan I offered to pay them back.

Now, I found plenty to pray about. Yet, very little to see as an adventure or life challenge that would make me learn about something or grow in.

In the evenings my son did everything he could to cheer me up. I tried for him but laughter had become a foreigner to my soul.

I did not see a way out.

I needed to make a choice to forgive Mack or move on without him in my life. I could not rationalize clearly.

Then, my memory took a strange twist. I started thinking the way I thought of him before I actually walked down the aisle and said 'I do'. I started to believe more of what he had said to me about myself. I started to hate myself.

I started believing that he actually was that man he promised me he was before our wedding. I thought of every time that he would make me feel less desirable and I would tell him to 'go after what he desired' when he looked at another woman. I started remembering every time I would hear him speaking gently to a woman on the phone and out of my desperation for him to talk to me with that same tone of voice I would ask him, 'why could he not talk to me the way he just talked to her?' I would reflect on the times that he would compliment with his attention and soft manners, another woman and allow them to be rude to me, but he would not stand up for me, making me feel worthless. I would at that time beg him to stand up for me and show me as much respect as he shows other women. He would get so angry with me and let me know that he never looked at other women, I was just jealous. He would get furious with me and let me know that he did not 'respect' other women and that it was just that I was a jealous bitch. He would rage at me in anger and when I pointedly asked him to stand up for me if and when someone else treats me horribly in front of him. He would smash things in his anger over me letting me know that he would not 'stand up' for a woman, that 'I could stand up' for myself. He said that it was only because I was such an insane, jealous, slut.

I was the cause for our marriage breakdown. 'He got along with everyone else in his life,' He would yell at me. 'Everyone else that knew him, loved him,' He would holler at me. I was the only problem in his life and it was all because I was a jealous bitch.

I would not remember that I had never been a jealous person before in my life. I could always appreciate a quality someone else had. After I got married ......I found out that I had no qualities at all.

He slammed my faith and told me how insane and stupid I was for it in so many ways. He would always be yelling at me that 'this was a sin,' or 'that was a sin.' He screamed at me in his car one time because while we stopped at a red light, he noticed that the two young men driving in front of us had started whistling and calling out to two young women standing at the corner bus stop beside us. Both of them looking like they could be for hire with very little money to do a man any favor he wanted.

"Look at that!" he screamed at me. "Those guys are sinning!"

"Mack, they may be single with no reason to be faithful to someone else." I told him in between the seething hate he was unleashing on me. "I am married and would not like to call out sexual things to a man, because I have you." He wasn't listening to me. "I don't think a man that is happy with a woman he has in his life needs to be crude and sexual with another woman." He didn't hear a word I said. He yelled and smashed the dash and door of his side of the car. He yelled at me how God should strike the two sinners in front of us dead.

The light turned green and he drove angry, rushing the rest of the way home. He had to get out of the car and away from me. He enjoyed admiring young women, never thought there was anything wrong with it; and I could not explain to him that the thing that bothered me the most…..was that I wanted to be enjoyed by my husband like he enjoyed other women. But; I was nothing to him.

He always refused to admit his interest in other women. Yet, you had to be deaf not to hear the difference in his voice as he spoke to them. You had to be ignorant if you didn't notice how he would laugh with them. You had to be blind if you didn't notice his respect for them. Finally, you had to be mindless if you didn't notice the different manner in which he yelled and screamed at me, and yet could not in any way upset (even in the smallest form) a stranger; if that stranger was a young woman.

He could scream and yell and swear at a man if he cut him off in a car or drove around him in a manner that ticked Mack off. But…..if it was a young woman driving…..then she could get away with the same action and he wouldn't say a word to her or show her that she made a mistake.

He could explode with a string of curses if it was directed at another man (and only if the other man was driving a car, never face to face). He could almost kill his son for pissing him off. He could almost kill me, but he would not show a young woman that she ever did anything wrong or upset him in anyway.

I stood before God and said for better or worse, till death do us part.

I stood before God and promised forever.

I stood before my family and friends and asked them to bless our union.

Before I completely threw Mack and me away, I would try one more time to do all I could for our marriage. I wanted to see if he was willing to change and be the man that he said he was before we got married. I would also see if I could change and learn how to completely forgive and learn how to love……"with no conditions".

I started phoning the crown council, writing letters and talking to anyone I could to fight for my husbands' acquittal. I would do what I could to see if the charges could be dropped. After that, it will be up to him as to what he wants to do.

'I' will do what I could to fight for my marriage. I was not responsible for what he wanted to do, whether that was to fight for us or throw us away. I just knew that if this marriage was to end, then I would be able to walk away saying …….'I did what I could'.

18

Loneliness

Mack had a good vacation with his mother, but when it was over and they were considering getting an apartment in the City, he started possibly thinking about the cost. (I don't know exactly what he thought, that is just going by the way I knew he had thought in other situations concerning money.)

We were not allowed to communicate with each other, yet Jason had received a phone call from his dad asking how I was doing. Jason asked me if I wanted him to know anything. I told him that he could tell his dad anything. I had nothing to hide.

Jason told his dad that we were praying for him and that I had a lot of people praying for our marriage. This was hard for Jason to do because at this point he no longer held any respect for his dad. Yet, Jason honored my request for him to believe with me in prayer for his dad's welfare.

I think this shocked Mack because the next day when he called Jason again he expressed a desire to come home. I told Jason to tell him that the only way he could was if he pled guilty. The worst that could happen to him, seeing as this was his first 'offence' was that he would get a nominal fine, but he would have a mark on his record. I found this out through many hundreds of phone calls I had been making since I got home with the camper. I wrote nonstop to the crown telling them that it was my fault, that I was sorry and requested that he please give my husband and I one more chance to see if we could still succeed in our marriage.

Two weeks later Mack was home. His mother had left back to Quebec and he only had to pay a $300 dollar fine.

I still vowed to never see his mother again. I would honor her wish to never see me again and prayerfully that would be the end of her in my life. Prayerfully the last time we had to look upon each other was the night she made that statement.

I purchased a marriage program and had hoped that instead of going to a 'group' for counseling, Mack and I could do something in the privacy of our home. I knew there was no way he would go to any counseling group anyway. He did not have any problems.......that is except me.

He brought me roses when he came home and we held each other all night long upon his first night back. He told me that he loved me and that he wanted 'us' to work. He never said sorry. He still believed that I deserved what I got from both his mother and himself that night, and quite frankly because of my low self esteem at that point; I didn't argue with him.

We discussed moving to an area where we could have a small farm and raise some animals. This was the first time that he was planning something with me. (Other than before we got married, but now looking back on that time; I knew that he never had any intentions of moving to Calgary and we ended up doing exactly what he wanted to do. He just had to take a little extra time talking to get it, but he got what he wanted. We got married and moved directly to Montréal and in with his parents.)

Things seemed to go rather well for that first week but when you have gone through that much emotional pain, well; you still have 'triggers'.

Once again he started talking rudely to me. Once again I started becoming nothing to him and he had quit the marriage course he began with me. He told me that 'I was the one that needed help' not him.

Again, I was the only problem. Once again my frail self worth started to surface.

His manner to me changed back to where I was 'walking on egg shells' and could not say or do anything that pleased him. He now had new ammo to throw at me also.

"It was because of me that he now had a criminal record." He started to yell at me how I had ruined his life when he got mad at me. He also hollered that he should have fought the charges and if he went to jail then it would be "a better life for him than to live with a bitch like me." I stood in the wrong spot. I couldn't read his mind fast enough and I asked him 'how his day went' when he would come home. The lists of my offences were pretty much a carbon copy of the ones I had obtained in Montréal.

I now once again believed he would be better off with someone else rather than me. Anytime he spoke to or showed interest or respect to another woman, I basically asked him…"what about her?" To myself I would ask, 'why doesn't he pursue her?' To Mack I would just let him know that I seen or heard his interest in them. I just didn't understand why he wanted to be with a woman that he hated so much and thought so very little about.

I was fighting every day to feel love for him. I searched the bible for a way out. But, my wounded mind just kept repeating….'for better or worse, in sickness and health, till death do us part.'

After I listened to him have a lengthy and enjoyable conversation with a secretary that he always talked to, I got hurt and ….yes…mad.

"Is she single?" I asked him when he got off the phone from laughing and talking with her for more than an hour and about more than just work.

He didn't waste any time in revolting at that statement and I went to work the next day covered in bruises. He never punched me but he definitely now grabbed me and threw me around along with the name calling when he got mad at me.

I caved from the mental strain and hearing all the talk about me at work. A supervisor of mine came up to talk to me when I was in charge of the med cart, handing out the morning pills. My uniform had short sleeves that could not cover the bruises. She stared at my arms and then quietly pulled me aside.

"Tammy, I am on my second marriage. My first husband was a very rude and angry man. He manipulated my children into hating me and used them against me any time he could. When I finally had the courage to escape the relationship I had to run and hide from him for several weeks. That meant I could not even tell my children where I was or why I left. He used that to let them think that I ran off with another man and abandoned them." She had pain with the memory of what she was confiding in me displayed in her eyes. "Tammy," she continued; "You are worth so much more than he treats you. One day you may find the courage to see that yourself."

I once again started coming to work crying, completely loathing who I was. I was a horrible slut, unworthy of love or respect. I deserved to be treated like scum. I no longer had any value.

Even my prayers seemed to disappear as soon as they left my lips. Could it be that God Himself had turned away from me too?

I quit my job, confirming to myself that Mack was right about me. I was a failure that could do nothing right.

After a month of looking for a farm, we found one and he bought it. It went into his name because it was his and was not going to be mine. He made that very clear to me.

I accepted this because I had no more fight in me.

206

We moved in February. The weather was horribly cold and blowing. The place we moved too had no drinkable water at that time but it would have when Mack got home. While it was snowing and blowing up here and I was unpacking; he had gone to Disneyland in California for just under a week. He told me he 'had' to go because it was his companies awards ceremonies. Even though he was not getting any awards, there was no way that he could possibly ask his employer for some time off to help me with this move. No, the sunny banquet was way more important than a freezing cold move. No wife's aloud. Or so he said. And even though we had the other place until the end of the month; Mack did not want to move in the cold and wanted to come home to a completely set up and unpacked house. He timed the move with his trip to California. It didn't matter.....it was only me.

So there I was again in a house with no money, no working phone, full of boxes, freezing cold, alone and no water to drink. I struggled to work with what I had and to unpack and clean the place before Mack got back from his sunny, warm trip.

My mother came to be with me for a couple of days but I had nothing to say anymore. I felt empty. She offered to go with me to get some groceries and bottled water from a small town close by. It was snowing heavy and the temperature was now at minus 40. We made it out of the long driveway and into town. I used what little money was in the account and came home with several bags mainly of no name drinks and no name cheep food items from the store.

On my way home we hit a large snow drift and the car was solidly stuck. We were instantly frozen as soon as we got out of the car. It was dark, snowing and just miserable that night. I tried desperately to dig the car out to no avail. I worked at it for almost an hour until I could hardly breathe anymore or feel my hands. I got into the car, closed the door and tried to phone Mack on my cell phone knowing that I only had a couple minutes worth of time on it left.

I was freezing cold, exhausted, and didn't know what to do.

He answered his phone and I could hear by the background noise that he was in a pub enjoying the warm weather and good company of his 'oh so important co-workers'. He apparently had just come back from watching a water show in Disneyland while eating a meal in one of their finer restaurants.

"Do you have time to talk?" I asked him.

"No. I just got finished watching a fucking boring water show. It was by a restaurant we ate at because 'I HAVE TO EAT', I am not having a good time and you bothering me is making my night worse." Anger laced his every word and I could tell by the laughter in the background that he wanted me off the phone. "Well? What the fuck do you want?"He wanted me to hear the inpatients with me in his voice.

I exploded. "I want money on my phone! I need to call AMA and I only have one more minute on my phone! Don't tell me you are not having fun! You can't wait to get me off the phone to go back to having a good time in sunny California with your co-workers and friends! The phone is going to run out of time! I need money on it now......and then if you don't want me in your life and want to have your fun.....THEN DIVORCE ME!!!!!!!!!!!!!!" I was so meaning that! The phone died. My body was shaking more from the cold but now because of the resentment that he honestly didn't give a shit about me! He was completely OK with me being in my situation because it was all about him. He was having fun with his co-workers doing exactly what he enjoyed the most. It didn't bother him in the least what I might be going through. It only bothered him that I had the audacity to interrupt that good time of his.

I told my mom that I wanted her to try walk to the house so she could at least by warm. I would walk with her and carry the groceries so they would not freeze in the car. If they did and I lost them then Mack would be incredibly mad at me for 'wasting his money' when he got home. I would need to make three trips, I calculated.

We left the car and started walking the rest of the way to the house. It was completely dark out now and definitely a night that you didn't even want your animals out in. It took us 20 minutes to finally reach the house. Once she was safely inside the house, I ran back to the car. I had to grab and lean on the hood to catch my breath before I grabbed more bags and do the trip again. I had to do this four times because I became so week and cold that I was stumbling because of exhaustion. The final trip took me forever. I finally fell to the floor in the house with the last bags and gasped and prayed for breath. I was shaking so much that I could not try to use the cell phone to see if Mack had put money on it. So, my mother worriedly used her cell phone and then gave AMA my cell phone number because it was going to use up all of her minutes also, and like me; she hoped that Mack put some money on it. We were both on 'pay as you use minutes' with telus mobility. Yet, we both knew that if she ran out of minutes and Mack didn't put more on my cell; then we were definitely going to be stranded until Mack came home.

Her minutes ran out while she was on hold with them. Then, my cell phone rang. I had my breathing more under control now and gave them the location of the car. They told me they would be with us in under an hour. I warmed up a little after the call and put warmer cloths on so I could go back out to the car to be there when they arrived.

I reached the car and grabbed the little shovel again to try to dig the car out. More just to keep moving so I didn't freeze than thinking that I was going to succeed.

AMA finally came and even he struggled to get the car out. It finally happened and two hours after phoning AMA, I was in the house, crying in bed and willing myself to actually start to warm up.

'I am glad you are having fun Mack,' I said to the ceiling.

'God ......help me please. I need you. I am so alone.' I prayed and sleep dragged me into a black hole of nothingness.

He never phoned me. According to him, he just never had time and it would cost too much to make a call anyway.

After Mack came home from that trip he informed me there was another trip being planned soon through his work. We got some dogs then later chickens. When the snow started melting we got quail, turkeys, geese, ducks, sheep and a horse.

Taking care of the animals became a full time job for me on top of which I got a job at a local gas station. The pay was almost not worth the gas it took to get there. However with that job plus taking care of the animals, I found that now I was too busy. Mack seemed to be always gone so I would be getting up before the sun, taking care of all the animals and then going to work only to come home in time to take care of the animals again just before I went to bed.

The animals saw me as their caretaker. They rarely seen Mack and when they did they would try to get away from 'the stranger'.

I did this for a couple months and maybe because I knew that Mack was getting his social needs met through his job and I got none of mine met, I quit at the gas station so I could concentrate on the hobby farm, on taking care of the animals. He was also going to hockey games paid for by his employer along with other entertainments. Not to mention going away to different places and leaving me be the house maid and animal caretaker.

I was just too mentally week to keep believing that this lifestyle was worth giving up my life for.

That is when the silence moved in. I would just sit after the chores were done and stare at …nothing.

My dad had passed away and Mack's response to that was…."he had been dying for a long time anyway."

I mourned him alone. Only the animals kept me company now. But at night for several months, I just sat on the deck alone in the evenings staring up into the sky. I felt for the first time that even my own life was slipping away.

I was still writing….it was my only out.

God, where are you in this place i find myself alone in space

i look for you in the secret place and see silence hide its face

i turn in hopes you have not gone and try to sing you a new love song

wishing in my darkest hour that you are still in complete power

you said in verse that all is yours and you would never leave

but in this as the night drags out without stopping………

i can't hear you for my heart pounding

God are you still with me or have i made you too unhappy

i can't seem to get things right, even when i try with all of my might

no where i turn or no matter what i do...things seem to elude me,

just like you

i know that i am not perfect and never will be.

but you promised your son to people just as stupid as me

the blind leading the blind you said .... were you thinking of me in that moment

you told us to be an example for you.... to be the hands and feet thats true

yet...my hands cannot create as you

and my feet often wonder to places i don't want them too

God are you there... can you still hear my cry... or have i done so much wrong that you no longer try

to give your ear to this, my plight in the night

or turn your eyes to see what i live in and
with and no longer care
it's as if i were not really even here....only you
know because i am so alone
in the middle of this unsure night.....that drags
itself on .... forever in site.

My son tried several times to get me to go out with him. He asked me to go for a hamburger or a drink at a one horse pub down the dirt road from our farm.

One day I finally did.

Jason and his girlfriend had moved in with us until they could find a place that would take them away from the big City. His girlfriend had gotten a job first and Jason had several interviews lined up for himself. It was a warm April day. Mack was going to make sushi for us all. He was working out of his home office that day, so he said he would slowly work on the dinner during his 'breaks'.

"Let's go for a game of pool mom." Jason begged me. "You have to get out of this house. You haven't done anything for almost a year!" He was talking about going to the one horse little pub near our place where you would be lucky to have maybe two or three people in there at its peak hours.

I finally relented, told Mack what we were going to do and then left with Jason in his car. I didn't feel too good about it because I knew that Mack hated me going or doing anything if he was home.

But, I went and I actually had a good time. I told Jason to text his dad to let him know that we had decided to stay out until Jason needed to go pick his girlfriend up after her work finished and then we would be coming right home after that. We were only about five minutes away from our farm down a dirt road anyway. We didn't think it was going to be a problem and I thought it was kind of nice to actually get out of the house for a change. It had been such a long time since I 'just went somewhere'.

After Jason and I left to pick up his girlfriend and make our way back to our place for dinner I was quite happy. I had drunk three coolers and two shots. That was way over my limit, but I laughed and told the kids that I would eat a lot for dinner then.

Then ....I felt something was going to happen. I became frightened like there was a dark brooding demon waiting/wanting to destroy me.

As we neared the farm's driveway I prayed for God to be with us. Then, the fear was replaced with sadness for another human soul (to this day I don't know who's, mine maybe? His?). Panic was replaced with a knowledge that I could call on God, even now.

I should have known not to have fun. I should have known not to leave the house. I should have known not to go anywhere with my son, and above all, I should have known not to want to laugh.

19

All in My Head

We had no time to get out of the car before Mack came running out of the house. He started cursing and swearing at all of us.

"YOU ARE A SLUT!" He pointed towards me, then Jason and then his girlfriend, "YOU ARE A SLUT AND SO ARE YOU!"

He screamed more fowl things at us then went back inside the house.

We walked up onto the porch not sure if we should go into the house too. Fear filled me for my son. There was no way he would be able to physically defend himself against his dad.

"We did text him didn't we Jason?" I tried to scan my brain to make sure that we told him where we were and what we were doing. I know we did, and his responding text back to us gave us no indication that he was upset with anything.

We heard him throwing and breaking things in the house.

I turned to Jason and looked him right in his eyes, "Don't try to fight him Jason!" I implored him more than commanded him not to try protecting anyone. "No matter what he does to me, you will not try to physically stop him Jason!"

I barely got that out of my mouth before Mack came hollering and yelling at me from the house again. I heard the door open as he came charging back out of the house.

I was about to turn towards him and the door when he shoved me with all his power off the porch. I let out a scream as I felt myself sailing over the porch steps in slow motion. I landed faster than I could possibly attempt to protect any part of my body in the fall. I hit the gravel hard and quickly tried to get up in a sitting position. He came down the stairs looming over me and yelling.

"What did I do!?" I cried out to him in anguish, "What did we do wrong?!"

I got up and tried to keep his attention as I seen my son and his girlfriend slip into the house. I later found out that he was trying to get his girlfriend away from Mack because she was absolutely terrified and crying.

Mack ran to the camper and I ran inside the house. As I ran into the house I could hear him breaking things in the camper.

I went into the back bedroom to make sure they were ok, and then raced out closing their door behind me because I heard Mack coming back into the house. I got to the kitchen the same time that he did.

"What did I do? What did we do wrong?" I begged him for an answer to his rage as he grabbed me and threw me across the room.

I got up again and he ran at me swearing and calling me every name he could think of in English and in French. He grabbed me again and threw me into the dining room. "Stop it Mack! We didn't do anything wrong!"

He came at me again when I was on my feet and with both of his hands and all of his might he pushed on my chest sending me backwards and I fell into the open guinea pig cage. It was a large two by four foot one we had on the floor. I had always kept the top open so I could pet him, now I wished I hadn't because while I was struggling to get out of it, I prayed desperately that I didn't land on him and kill him.

I was struggling to get out of the now bent cage and saw Jason and his girlfriend come out of their room. Terror came over me at the thought of Jason trying to fight his dad.

216

I called to Mack as I pushed myself up and away from the cage to get his attention hoping that he would keep his anger focused on me and not see Jason or his girlfriend.

"I am going to call the police if you don't stop!" I yelled at him.

He swung around again and ran at me from the living room where he was smashing things.

His nose was almost touching mine as he handed me the phone. "Go ahead you slut, bitch, fucking useless, miserable, insane SLUT!"

I grabbed it and noticed that it had been thrown already and there was a couple pieces missing. I also noticed that Jason and his girlfriend must have gone back into their room because they were nowhere in sight.

I dialed 911. I had to get Mack away from the kids.

Mack went deadly silent, put his middle finger up and placed it on my nose and between my eyes while I was on the phone.

"Are you safe ma'am?" 911 questioned me.

"My husband and I had a fight…." Mack pushed his finger harder into my face and mouthed the words slowly, F…U…C…K…..Y…O…U! Then he turned around and went and sat on the couch staring at me.

"I was going to phone you about a fight with my husband …." I didn't want him arrested again but I did want him to stop his hate and anger…"but he went to sleep and is sleeping now. He was drunk and yelling but everything is ok now. I am sorry for phoning you, goodbye." I hung up not taking my eyes off of him. You could almost see the hate and anger dripping of his body. His eyes were completely black. He slowly started to get up and walk towards me……then the phone rang.

I answered it when he was about two feet away from me.

"Hello?" My eyes never left his.

"Ma'am, this is 911; you cannot just hang up on us."

"I am sorry." I had to get them off the phone. I had to stop this anger, and wanted everyone just to go to sleep so nothing more happened this night.

I don't know how or what I said but the phone was once again on the table.

Mack lunged at me. I went flying across the room and he raced into the kitchen. He grabbed a large butcher knife, swung around and came at me with the knife gripped in his fist and aimed at my gut.

Time stopped.

He was swearing and running at me in slow motion.

"This is how I am going to die?" I wasn't asking anyone, it was more like a realization of that was all the time on this earth that I had. I was not going to have any more to my life story. The details would be in the paper. Then my name would disappear from this world. This was how it was going to end.

He was driving the knife through the air towards my stomach. As my head lowered to watch the knife now just two inches from my gut, I thought, "what about my son!"

"JESUS HELP!" I don't know if I cried to Jesus out loud or just screamed HIS name in my head, but Mack stopped instantly.

There was an absolute picture of mass confusion on his face and he all of a sudden didn't know what he was doing. He stepped back and looked down at the knife in his hand. He turned it towards himself and then screamed at me that he was going to kill himself.

I knew he wasn't going to. But time resumed to a normal fast pace. I grabbed the knife from him and threw it into the living room. (God must have done that because I would not have been able on my own to get the knife away from him.) He stumbled back. He didn't know what he was doing. He looked around knowing that he had a knife but didn't know what happened to it and then he swung around to run into the kitchen to get another one.

I thought, "This isn't going to end tonight and I had to make it stop!"

I ran to the room where Jason and his girlfriend were and swung open the door. "PHONE the police!" I saw that his girlfriend was sobbing in terror and Jason was holding her close to himself. He was already talking to 911. I slammed the door closed and ran back to the kitchen to keep Mack from coming down the hallway.

I watched him standing in the kitchen sorting through the knives amongst the broken sushi plates that he apparently threw everywhere. He was confused. He looked up at me and backed away. He turned and ran out of the house towards the camper and jumped inside slamming the door behind him.

Jason and his girlfriend came out of the room. They started to talk to me but I couldn't really hear them. I could see the anger and frustration on Jason's face.

I went to my bedroom that was just off the dining room and sat on the bed wincing in pain. My arm. Something happened to my arm. When? How?

Jason and his girlfriend were by my side and I seen through the windows a red and blue light emerge slowly and then get brighter. Those lights filled the room, the house, my thoughts……my world turned into red and blue lights. My son was talking to me but I no longer heard him. I sat there grabbing my left arm and not moving.

"It is over."

The police came into the house and noted all the broken glass and tossed furniture. Jason showed them the guinea pig cage. He and his girlfriend were talking to them but I couldn't seem to follow their conversation. I wanted to disappear.

Mack was in the camper. He was going to get arrested again.

For what? Because we were not here when his sushi was ready? We weren't sitting at the table five minutes before it was ready to be placed on the table? Every time we ate sushi there was always left over's that we would eat cold the next day. It was a meal that would not go bad or need to be served right away. The food was not going to be 'destroyed' or 'wasted'. Was it because I went out with my son? I haven't done anything that took me away from this farm except work at the gas station and help three times at the little local pub. Was it because I did something without him? Did he hate his son that much!

I didn't know who he was. I never knew what would piss him off. He had rules for me, but none for himself. I could be put down and hurt but I was not to even dream of saying even the tiniest of things to upset him.

On the rare occasions that I cooked a meal and called to him that it was ready; he didn't immediately stop what he was doing to race to the table. He finished what he was doing and then came to eat. To me, this was not a big deal. A meal could still be appreciated even if you let it cool down a bit because you want to finish something or take time to clean yourself up before coming to the table.

I got drunk one night and threw a temper tantrum like one of his. I picked things up and threw them around the house. I called him a pig stuffed with vanity and ego. I told him he was the epitome of selfishness. I told him to go fantasize about young girls. Then I chucked a large candle that hit one of the dining room glass shades breaking it. I finally told him to get out. I kept yelling for him to get out until he finally did. He jumped into his car and took off.

220

He text me and told me that he did not want to live with a person like that.

I took a risk. I played with fire. I wanted him to see what I see and listen too almost daily from him. It could have turned violent instead of just me ranting but for some reason he just watched me almost pleased with himself. It was like he was relieved that now he could tell the truth to people and let them know what a raving lunatic he married.

"That is the type of person I live with Mack almost every day or every time I do something small to piss you off." I was horrified that he didn't see it. He ignored that statement and just reaffirmed to me that he didn't want to live with that type of person. He told me that 'if' he acted like that it was because I must have pissed him off.

Really?! That still didn't make sense to me. This told me that it was perfectly acceptable in our marriage for him to throw temper tantrums? 'If' that reaction was a good marriage building action; then didn't it make it right for me to react the same way? I didn't want to and I wanted him to stop them too.

No, he informed me he wasn't going to stop until I never pissed him off again. Simple; if I never wanted to see his temper then just stop pissing him off. It was perfectly fine for him to show rage and anger when 'I deserved it'. To which he informed me that he never deserved a wife that had a temper.

"Fine." I stated without emotion. There was nothing I could do or say. He wanted to believe that he was a victim in our marriage and that he never, ever, ever did or said anything wrong or that I did not deserve.

He came back the next day as if nothing happened.

I was lost. Mack did things that he apparently never did. It was all in my mind. He said things that he never said. It was all in my mind. He showed me and told me often how much he hated me. yet, if I asked him why or told him what he said to me....his response was ..."I never said or did that, Tammy; it is all in your fucking head!"

I sat on the bed. All his anger was just in my head. I was 'imagining' everything because he did no wrong.

The police walked out of the house and walked right to the camper. I don't know what he said to Mack or really what happened at that point except they handcuffed him and took him away again.

Epilogue

I fought again for him. I spoke to the crown counsel, phoned people and worked with the help of victim services. I did not want to see him go to jail. I wanted him to be the man I married. The man he told me he was before I said "I do." I knew he had it in him because I seen how he spoke to and interacted with others. The man I knew that loved people. The man that couldn't do enough for you, and loved to see someone happy and laugh because of something he did or said. That was just one side of him, but it was the side that I fell in love with and dreamed about as my soul mate.

I was not making an excuse for his temper or encouraging him to continue to think that he could hurt me just because he was mad and in his mind I deserved his wrath. I did want him to understand that even though some people may allow him to treat them badly and just accept that 'that is Mack'; it is wrong to think it is right just because he gets away with it.

God never made us Judge and Jury. Even in 'our' physical world those tasks go to multiple people working together to acquit or convict a person and finally hand out reward or punishment.

Slowly though, a new reality hit me. There was a deeper understanding of something that I made reference to over the years of our marriage yet now for some reason, it had fully dawned on me; and it wasn't a comfortable realization.

Mack was his dad. Before his dad was placed into 'a home' and before he became completely dependent on medication and care of a medical staff to live. His dad needed to be right and had little tolerance with imperfection, either in himself or others that were close to him. He couldn't just watch someone do something in a way that he thought was 'wrong' or 'not his way'. He would step in and take over. His short term memory, like an old record was skipping. This created havoc in his mind because he hated to fail, and not remembering where he put something equated failure to him within himself. This in itself spurred him on to rationalize that someone else must have moved 'it'; it had to be 'someone' else's fault. He hated looking for something, not finding it and then finally asking/demanding that you find it for him; then realize that it was right in front of his vision. This happens to all of us and is 'normal' but to someone in the very early stages of a type of dementia, it happens almost daily.

I started to see the same mannerism and forgetfulness that I saw in his dad years earlier appearing more often in Mack. I was watching the same character form. The very words he spoke with intolerance and anger; was his dad years earlier. I listened to him repeating himself, telling the same joke or story many times over. This is the hardest time for people on both sides of the fence because it doesn't make sense. People will question themselves and can't understand the confusion that comes with any type of dementia. I knew that often the person going through it can't see it in themselves. The only thing the person may know with early stages dementia at this point is:

1. They may get frustrated much easier than they ever had before in their life
2. They may loose their patients much sooner than they remember they ever had
3. They may get angrier faster ….or….. they may give up on things sooner than they used to (this part really depends on the personality of the person before any type of dementia starts; some people

withdraw into themselves and start to lean more and more on those around them; where as some people react to the changes fighting and pushing people away.)

4. Some people have a 'feeling' of 'I should be doing something' or 'I was going to do something, but what'. (It would be like me waking up in the morning feeling anxious or stressed because 'I over slept for work or an appointment', then slowly realize that I hadn't and it could even be one of my days off of work.)

5. This may lead them to ...'keep busy' by going from one job to the next leaving the majority of these projects unfinished and then feeling 'overwhelmed' with a huge 'to do' list that is sometimes only in their mind. (This may be why, whenever I wanted to talk to my husband about things that we needed to do; he would immediately get mad. In his mind he probably already had the sense of being overwhelmed with 'things to do' and I was just adding to them. Mack's dad had many things started yet hardly any of it finished.)

They didn't forget they moved something; someone else must have moved it on them. Inanimate objects can incur their harsh wrath because 'it' wasn't co-operating. And, finally; out of their frustration they needed to 'vent'. They can't vent to the world; then the world would see their turmoil and unveil their faults. In moments of unease (or confusion) for Mack's dad in a public (or private) setting, he would start to mimic others. If he seen everyone laughing, then he would laugh also even if he don't know what was supposed to be funny. If he was walking with you and you stopped to look at something, he would show the same interest without knowing why the object or subject would be interesting (this of course is more pronounced later as the disease progresses).

The 'safe' people in their lives they feel they can release anger and frustration on is a spouse or children.

Of course this is 100% wrong. No one needs to submit to another person's unreasonable anger. The only hope I had was that now I understood. I had hope because I started to see the end of the tunnel of questioning my own sanity. The 'hope' I had was the knowledge that I was not going insane. Now, I knew what I was dealing with. It was more than a man with an unrealistic, uncontrollable temper. It was with a man that very possibly was going to end up like his dad; in a home for persons with dementia, on medication and needing complete care one day.

This realization did nothing to ease how I felt with how he dealt with me. It didn't stop the loneliness and pain I was living in.

Unfortunately, the answer didn't come until one year after I had taken him back into my life. He was put on probation for three years with several 'conditions'. If he broke any of the conditions or the Judge heard that he had hurt me again, then the Judge quite clearly stated to Mack that he would be once again looking into 'his' eyes (meaning that he was going to be the Judge to sentence him even if he happened to be on vacation and Mack had to sit in jail to wait for him to return). Then the Judge promised Mack he would go directly to jail and serve his whole sentence.

So what this meant for Mack was that he had 3 years to prove that he would not hurt me again. He had three years to prove that he could manage his anger in a normal and more constructive way. If he did hurt me during that time; the suspended sentence would come forward and Mack would go to jail for 5 years.

There were people that wanted to call the police on him again on different occasions since the Judge said that to him. I included myself in that group a couple times, but knew that I would not be able to stop him from going to jail again.

So, I let him continue to shove me around, call me names and throw his temper tantrums breaking whatever he decided he wanted to break. And that was generally my things not his.

I had to wait for clarity of my mind through a cold, lonely year.

My truck had broken down and Mack was busy with his job. My world consisted of complete silence within the walls of this old house. My only companionship were the animals living with me on the farm.

When Mack was around I had to sit, stand, do, speak, shut up and roll over only when he gave me the authority to do so. He was going to make me pay. I had to pay for anything he thought was my fault. Even the very decision he made in wanted to marry me. I especially had to pay for that! Even though…..(again)….it was a choice he made to ask me, but somehow, from right across Canada; I made him marry me against his own will.

I struggled with the loneliness and isolation. I hardly read my bible or prayed. Several times I broke down and thought I would go insane if I didn't get out of this house, there was a few times I completely exploded in frustration towards Mack, at being unwilling to love me.

One of those moments was when once again in the coldest part of the year after the Christmas season; Mack was in sunny, warm Texas with his co-workers. My thoughts centered on the fact that he was able to get out of the house and breathe. He was able to live and socialize. He was able to forget about me and live for himself.

I phoned him and yelled at him in an unreasonable desperate manner.

"I want a divorce!" I knew that I was asking for something that he wouldn't mind giving me but he also told me that he couldn't afford to give me one. I knew, the real reason was because in order for him to have his job, live his life the way he wanted to and keep a hobby farm running was to have a 'caretaker' that he didn't have to pay. He needed to keep me on his farm to work/take care of it and this also allowed him to know exactly where I was and what I was doing while he was living his life.

The one part of me that didn't mind this (and only part of me) was the fact that I loved the animals and wanted to see them cared for properly.

A blessing that came from that explosion was his interest in ice fishing when he came back from Texas. He took me on day trips to nearby lakes, and although we never caught anything the whole season; I loved to get out of the house. I didn't care if we ever caught a fish, I just loved doing it.

Finally, I started to pray and read my bible again.

Through scripture and prayer I started looking at myself. I started to see clearly that I needed to focus more on how I was reacting to him and understood that I also needed to learn what it meant to 'love unconditionally'.

It wasn't about changing Mack. It was now about changing me.

A penny for your smile my dear,

said the passerby.

He held a bag of change and waved it in the sky.

You make the sun brighter, and the stars dance at night
when you show your pretty grin, it all works out just right.
Even when problems come and darkness fills your day,
A smile to someone you don't know,
washes cares away.
Through the tears of sorrows years,
I lifted up my chin
And gazed into this strangers eyes,
where there was no sin.
His love streamed over me, and comfort soothed my soul
I knew at once what he said would fill my empty hole
A hole that came from crying, had pierced my heart through.
Yet in those words of wisdom I knew it all was true.
I fell at his feet and clung to his robe,
Into the very depth of me his searching eyes did probe.

He knew I had it in me, or he would not have
asked me to,
So leaning on his strength, hope and vision
came anew
I knew he'd give me his reward if his request I
do.
I smiled at first weakly, then joy filled my
empty heart
He handed me the penny saying this is for
your brand new start.
A penny for your smile, I said to a passerby,
Holding up the one I had and waved it in the
sky.

Who knows how long he has before more of his
dad's character shows itself in him. I just know that I now
started loving myself again. I started to trust God again. I
could breathe again.

I also knew that it wasn't his family that I never
wanted to see again or care about. I knew that it was only
Mack's angry words that created a distance and dislike
between his family and my son and I. It wasn't them or me.
I was able to forgive them and him. I was able to care
again.

I would always love Mack with an unconditional
love, but only God knows if I will be able to help him walk
down the path that he was surely going.

On a Personal Note

I don't want to tell you how my story ends. I don't even know myself but, I don't want you to know if I left or stayed and have someone use that to make a choice for themselves that only they can make.

If you're going through something like this, then 'you' are the only one that can make that choice. 'You' are the only one that knows your heart, your circumstances and how safe you are in that relationship.

I know some amazing women that had to leave their relationships for their own safety or sanity. I love them and believe that they made the right choice. I also know of other women that have 'stuck it out' and stayed. They too are also wonderful women that have given me strength to go through what I had to. None of them made the 'wrong' choice.

No one can tell you what to do. And if you are a counselor reading this….please….PLEASE…. I beg you….understand that it is more important to support a woman's decision to stay or go, rather than just saying….'go'. Please remember, we do love these men (the men that promised us the moon covered in a forever after romantic love), and need help learning how to value ourselves, then we can make a decision that we can feel good about. Then, we can decide to stay or go. Then, we can live again and most importantly….love again.

To learn how to ….'love'….ourselves again.

Some women need to leave and some need to learn that they are not the only one in the relationship with needs and wants. The strange thing about filling someone else's needs is that sometimes we 'need' to put our own needs aside, fill theirs and ours amazingly are all of a sudden met.

We can change a mind....our mind....or someone else's mind....but we can't change someone's heart.

My husband went through 'anger management counseling'. It did not change him.

It changed him long enough to get the 'letter of good behavior' from the instructing counselors. He knew to repeat exactly what they wanted him to say so he could get that important...'letter confirming his "co-operation" in class.

Somehow my husband came out of the course confirming his belief that 'I was the only one with the problem' but "he could only change himself, not his messed up wife." He took what he wanted to take out of it and apparently left the rest in the class room.

Anger Management courses differ depending on who is teaching it. I know of one in particular that is taught by an amazingly compassionate team of people. They do follow up with the spouse and check in with the participant after they have finished the course. Their course is not only about managing anger but helping the person deal with some of its sources. One of those sources is having 'control' issues. I believe that the course this particular team leads has helped people.

The most disturbing thing about the course my husband went through is that there was no follow up with the abused spouse to find out if the abuse has actually stopped.

The people going through the course know what hate and anger mean, they need to learn more about what 'love' means.

Love is the first and second commandment. Unconditional love is the hardest yet easiest love to give. It was hard when I realized that unconditional love means I love someone based on choice, not what they do, or do not do; to, or for me. It became easy when I finally understood this. It became easier when I learned how to give it, and I felt the freedom it brought to me. Emotional freedom is amazing!

There are so many different circumstances to each of our own stories.

I found strength in reading my bible and learning how to make God my hiding place. He really is my strength in times of weakness and my wisdom in times when I know nothing.

When I think about Joseph being imprisoned because of a lie; I think about how he dealt with it. He trusted that God was still in control. Joseph went through a time in his life as the lowest of the low. Yet God rewarded him by making him more powerful than anyone else in the Kings court. He was then able to help his family and save them all from famine.

I wish I could say I was as faithful during my 'prison' sentence (that is how I felt living in isolation from love). I am ashamed that I cannot. I failed miserably and cried many nights because of my own vanity and sorrow. That is, until I realized that I was not in my battle alone. I had Jesus.

He never left me. He brought me through the Valley a stronger woman.

I 'TURNED THE STONE THAT WAS MEANT TO CRUSH ME, AS A STEPPING STONE TO GO HIGHER!"

I am thankful that the Lord taught me what 'unconditional love' really means. In understanding this type of love, I am able to understand with more depth the love that he has for me.

I pray that no matter what trial you are going through right now, that you will have someone to lean on.

All my love to you, the reader of my story.

About the Author

Born in Kelowna British Colombia, the author spent most of her childhood in central BC. She is a Mental Health and Special Needs Worker, with over 20 years experience in that field. Having since traveled to many places in Canada, the US and beyond, she is now settled down in central Alberta. She is a mother to one (who she raised as a single parent from his birth to grade 12), and now the beloved grandmother of a beautiful baby girl; and married to her first love.